\<THE UNNAMED WORK\>

By

\< Rachel Lorelai Villanueva \>

ISBN: 978-1-965190-31-9

...The journey toward ending your suffering...

<<You'll never escape polarities; of desired & unwanted but you do choose its perception>>

You don't need to travel away to a retreat, follow a certain lineage & leave your family or go to the deepest jungles, NO THE TIME IS NOW available to you!! In this book, I'm sharing my program that will give you practical tools to use and shift your consciousness and the use of spirituality to empower you in your daily life. Wherever the struggle is in family, work, relationships, physically, mentally or emotionally ... where you want to grow and change it is all possible and given to you NOW.

<Rachel Lorelai Villanueva>

Psychic, spiritual & yoga teacher.

"You need to die first while you are still alive, to live a life that is meaningful and purposeful"

If you turned the pages and you are reading this, you are on the right track and Yes this is a sign of the Universe; that you are holding this right now, even if you are still wondering whether this book is for you...

All the steps, and synchronicities have brought you right here, right now. And while we hear so much about many different modalities, paths and journeys in spirituality, the Unnamed work will be your guide and help you dive into various healing and transformational aspects of your life. Because you are so unique and this work is so unique it will remain unnamed... Same as no one can put a name on you, or put you into a box... If you want to learn about how you can be the alchemist of your life, the magician of unexplained situations or simply be Free of pain; because you understand its polarities in any of its shapes or forms, you have come to the right place. Take this key and dive with me into the Unnamed work; lets open together the doors of how we can learn to surf on the waves of suffering rather than being crushed by it...

Rachel Lorelai Villanueva

This Book Is Dedicated To Life Itself

Acknowledgment

You reading this right now.

All the ones I know, who know me, to the ones that hurt me intentionally or unintentionally, thank you.

Without any trauma or past experiences, I would have no story to tell nor share, which in the end became and birthed my teachings to share for you, a tool for you to use. To hopefully be a guide in your spiritual journey in order for you to leave and end your sufferings behind you.

To the brave ones who left the matrix and the illusion and fought for the right to live a life that is meaningful, joyful & purposeful. To the ones who were brave enough to step into the unknown and who had the courage and willpower to shift and consciously create their own reality. I thank you to life itself, who showed me that there is more to life than just where you were born, where you live, and where you survive. To be able to see above higher perspectives beyond just the materialistic, capitalistic way of seeing life. To the ones that trust their inner compass and believe that abundance, health, and all the magic life can give is a mere reflection of what you decide to create and put your attention towards. How to access or achieve anything you desire or dream in life is something that has always been inside of you. So, thank you, haters, family, friends, and co-workers. Thank you also to you mom & dad. For all of my experiences from childhood to adulthood, for all, I have learned, picked up, and decided what was to be kept or left behind.

To my brother, thank you for being the light in the dark. For our joyful, funny, or sad experiences, enabling us to see that the crazy waves above the sea level and the silent calm deep sea below are one and the same ocean.

Thank you, Stacey, for you were the very first person to start my program about the teachings of the Unnamed Work, which brought you to the journey of healing and the path toward ending your suffering. You hold a special place in this.

Stephanie, my best friend, thank you for all the love, support, laughter, and tears throughout the years; I believe our journey needed to start with the white lady...and go toward infinity and beyond.

My deepest gratitude goes to my Ninong Herman and Tita Doris; they are the embodiment of living life to the fullest with so much independence, love, and passion. Thank you for the wisdom. I hold it preciously in me.

To Ate Cecil and Christy, thank you for showing me what it means to be powerful and brave and to go for your dreams; you both are a true inspiration to me.

But mostly and lastly, thank you Daniel, the alchemist, the chameleon and creator you are. You are the very reason that pushed me faster to jump into the unknown. The mirror reflects back at me, reminding me where I needed to grow and evolve. For my expansion as well as for your own, a path we have walked in love, creativity, and consciousness itself to hold the infinite space for it all.
Thank you, from my heart.

Table of Contents

Introduction

You needed to face the deepest pain and the possibility of dying, in order to wake up of the dream...

#

Is life made this way? That you need to feel the deepest pain, the hurt, the depression, the sickness, or the heartbreak? It is always in the unknown, or when we are standing face to face with being abandoned or insecure, that we recognize something is just not going right. You can't go on living your life this way. Once you have been ripped off that easy train ride, you cannot jump back into the mundane life you had before that darkness ripped you off of your dream. It is almost as if we could see life as a journey, a ride where you jump in that train and it rides smoothly to its destination. You have many stops where you get out and enjoy the view, each time in a different place. Different people, different situations...almost as a normal and regular easy-going ride, usually a bit similar; very known, very familiar. Getting in and out of the train with

1

its many stops, again, again and again. As you sit on your well-known chair, on your well-known mind. Until this major emergency break, when everyone gets kicked out of that train. What the fuck just happened here? You were on this chill way of living, day to day, seeking weekends and holidays, enjoying your life until none of that was longer important. In this discomfort, you start to search for distractions such as television, sex, social media, food, alcohol, drugs...Anything! Anything to numb this pain. Anything to numb what is going on, this life off track, this unknown painful kick of life, where now you are just lost. You wonder and ask yourself what is the meaning of life. No one can understand you, yet all you want is to be understood, seen, connected and loved. Or maybe you just want your health back, or you want to go back to before that train stops. But you can't; they have moved on, and life seems to move on, with or without you. It seems as if you were the crazy one, or is it them? This is a time of extreme, a time of crisis, a time of unknown... and this is where the Unnamed work falls on your lap to accompany you in these unknown times...

It is no coincidence you fell on this book; you might have been searching and questioning, but you have arrived. I got you. There is a way out of that hell you currently are experiencing, no matter how that hell looks like to you or them. For some, it may also be a golden castle keeping you caged, the repeating shit happening to you, the wanting and longing for better health, the grasping to feel good again, to have peace of mind and heart, or simply the wanting and wishing, yet nothing is happening. Nothing is changing. You see on social media how they rub their money, happiness, and health on your face...How about I tell you there is a way to transform all of that? Mostly, when we don't understand something, we turn in circles. Or we repeat and try similar things again and again with the expectation of getting different results each and every time. Yet nothing changes, and not only is that insane, but it is driving you insane, too! When you start to understand a pattern, you can modify it. You might think that you are stuck at some level, but if you bought this book and are willing to transform to change, then it means there is another way. It also means you are exactly where you need to be, right here, right now, even if it doesn't make any sense yet. There is a possibility of you getting the life you want, the dreams you have, the shifts and goals you aspire to in your life. Here is how these teachings will change your life for the better and how you can finally change what needs to be resolved in order for you to truly own your life and your potential. A client I was once talking to in my living room has said: I have been going many years to a psychiatrist who kept on telling me the same thing again and again. You need to leave it behind and walk through the door... That's easy to say! How do I walk through that door? She kept on falling and reviving the old patterns and pain. Only after the teachings was she grateful beyond words. As she said, I finally got the key. The key to open that bloody door and finally step through it. That is what I can see for you, too, as you read this and are grasping for that missing link. It will not be an easy road, that I know, but at the point you are right now, how worse could it get? If you dive into this work rigorously, you will not go back to who you were before; you will become free. Free from all the thoughts and self-made prison in your head. I can promise you that you will discover how much power lies in you, your mind, your innate capacity, and how to work in symbiosis with the sacred temple we call the physical body. In this work, you will be introduced to a multifaceted array of tools and ways for understanding, reconnecting within, healing, growth, expansion, and integration with very powerful combined techniques no one really talks about. All of these are just some of the picks of what we will together unravel in this book. Your vision will be like that of an eagle, sharp and with a high perspective from above. This new set of eyes will allow you to connect with the metaphysical and mystical. You will start to see above the noise and beyond all of the illusions and filters that have veiled your Reality for so long. By all means, not in an ego way of being better than them, or you being "awakened" and them "asleep". This is not about choosing camps...But rather unveiling your strength, and intuition and recognizing that inner essence and light. The interconnectedness of All things in existence, instead of all the divided camps we see today. How you can become untouchable because you simply see Love in All things. And if this all sounds airy-fairy, I speak from a place of experience because the hell you are going through, I went one myself, where I needed to experience dying in this waking lifetime, and my love for truth and understanding is one of the many reasons this book came to life for You.

Since I was a child, I have always been questioning and interested in social behaviors. When something was "not ok" or how you are not supposed to "behave" that way in society, I was the first one trying it out, and then I questioned why. Which I must say, pretty got me a lot of times "in trouble". Today, I see it all as a gift. Because of that, I was able to discover what questioning really meant. Which brought me later to deconstruction. A technique that you will be learning, too. For it has always been my curiosity and questions about life that got me into wanting to understand beyond the physical. As a child, I could tap into divinatory dreams, dreams of the past and future; I just thought that was something normal. When someone in my family had aches, they asked me to massage them and help them release stuck energies and heal them. But what really got me to dive into spiritual work was the ignorance of some other people who transmuted pain into an indescribable act of violent words and hurtful behaviors, where I could find no understanding of where that came from. Nor the reason from where all pain and negativity came from. Growing up in a religious family, there were some questions that could not be answered or asked. Why would there be an aspect of darkness and pain if god created it all and was all loving for all his creation? For questioning religion, you were weird or disrespectful. Hell and heaven, evil and good, it just made no sense; why would one reject others and judge others? That was the first time I went down the path of spirituality because I just wanted to understand what had never been explained to me or what no one could give answers... But as I said, it is mostly in phases of traumatic experiences. You get ripped off that train. These many situations and traumatic events shape and push you to evolve. But the biggest wake-up call was the fight I needed to have with myself. I needed to face the deepest pain and the possibility of dying, as my body and my health were seemingly abandoning me. I went through endless doctor visits and multiple tests as I was struggling with digestion issues. Doctors kept saying that maybe it was just stress, but maybe I was making this up in my head. Scapegoating and gaslighting me, to a point, I started to question my sanity and if something really was wrong with me or if I was really just making this up. After two years of struggle, I was merely skin on bones. And I thought, this is it; I'm going to die. At thirty, taking seven different medications daily, I thought of writing a testament and started to think about a bucket list. The main message I want to say here, with this story that happened years ago, is that in my deepest pain, struggle, and darkness, I have found the light within. As said, my journey with spirituality and the mystical and psychic abilities as a child has always, in some shape or form, been present in my life, but I know for sure that these capabilities are innate in every one of us humans. The dormant part just needs to be re-awaken, and its full potential needs to be reminded of. And so, it is the same with starting to dive into spiritual work or the metaphysical aspects and questions of our reality. But it is in the darkest alley of our personal journey, in times of pain, trauma, or sickness, that we do get ripped out of the mundane road and kicked into realizations of life and the meaning of life itself. In all of that pain, shadow, or negativity lies tremendous information about yourself. To me, in that pain and darkness lies the gem, the power to unravel the potential we humans carry within. Today, I am free of any medication; I have healed myself physically and mentally through my own spiritual practices. I found the key no one could give me at that time, and I want to share it with you. Physical healing is just a tiny aspect of what you will learn with the teachings of the Unnamed work.

This book is your key, your guide, to be used and modified as your very own spiritual practice. I'm just reminding you of the ancient wisdom and knowledge you had in you all along. I invite you to use this as a recipe, but one that you can turn into your own personal one, where you incorporate your very own unique taste and flavors. This is not a self-help book that you read once and forget about it. I wish for you to take this as a lifestyle you adopt into your day-to-day life. It is to be taken as your new way of seeing life, your new way of filling your cup. Part of what I teach is to remind you of how powerful we all are but also to dive into the controversy, to go out of the box and break the glass ceiling. To me, it is our birthright to be creative, intuitive, and free people; freedom is and should be our way of being and living life. But our current social system, with its daily duties, sacrifices, paying bills, supporting, and providing, has made us caged and forget why we came here. Taming the untamed wildness in us...And it is only when the uncomfortable becomes so unbearable that we seek change. When every cell in our body shouts enough is enough, but instead, we behave as we should, we sacrifice as expected. I want to provide you with this lens to show that there is another way of looking at and understanding life. But like any hard work you want to achieve in life, it takes courage, bravery, strength, patience, and the belief that you will get there no matter who or what. This is not a quick fix or a shortcut. To me, that does not exist. Therefore, it is called the dark night of the soul journey. Because you climb up and down, there are many seasons and different changes of view and scenery. It starts mostly from dark painted colors, but as you continue walking, you unveil more and more the colors of the planets, the colors of this vibrant life that has many, many spectrums and dimensions. You will arrive at some point safely to death; the only question is how you get there and what is your legacy.

And in this dark night of the soul journey, you have to start somewhere. As I said, if you have been turning in circles and nothing is changing, there is a first step to take, and that is to recognize it. You no longer want to live this way; you no longer want to feel alone, sick, broken, sad, or abandoned. But in order to go towards what you want to create, you need to start a ritual; you need to de-program limiting beliefs of not being good enough or shame and the deep wounding of the trauma you went through. And that is just what we are going to start in the first coming chapters. How important it is to have healthy lifestyle rituals the moment you wake up and get out of bed. So that your habits become your new way of showing up, and your values become the truth that shapes your personality, your reality, and the essence you transmit out to the world. With no further due, I let you dive into the first chapter, where you will meet "mala ritual" and conscious meditation in order to shift, reprogram, and affect matter through energy with the force of your consciousness. With gratitude and love, I thank you for letting me be your guide in this journey. Make tea and sit back. Let's use this key, open the doors together, and dive into the unnamed work.

Chapter One

Your Morning Rituals and Conscious Meditation

#

How do you start your day? You get up, stretch, go to the bathroom, and then direction to the kitchen for coffee, cocoa, or tea, whatever your choice is. Think about your morning routines. It is the very base start that sets the tone for the coming day. You know that waking up late, in a hurry, stuck in a traffic jam can all be retraced about how your very morning started. Which in turn affects your entire day. The interactions you will have with the people around you, in the business workspace or wherever you plan your day to be, all start with the way the tone of the day was set. Will you be more irritated, tense, aggressive, impulsive, or angry? Or is your mood going to be joyful, good, relaxed, light, and playful, no matter what? Usually, when you go to work every morning or do whatever you do, each morning has the same ritual. You could basically copy past yesterday into today or tomorrow. So, what does your blueprint look like that you create, and does it turn into a routine each day upon getting up?

What is important to know before diving further into these rituals is that what you do is based on how you are habituated. A practiced behavior becomes a habit, second nature, till, in the end, such an automatism is reflected in becoming your new personality. This is why it's so important and essential to have a daily set of routines. If you hear yourself again and again wondering why you overreacted again or why the right words or actions were not done, maybe it's time to dive deeper into your psyche and start changing that blueprint. This is done daily, no matter what, the same way you wash your body daily and brush your teeth. This is now your new part of a ritual to cleanse your mind and soul, aka your three bodies (I.e., your physical body, astral body, and spiritual body).

In order to have a little ritual of your own, it is nice to have a Mala, which is a 108-beads necklace, as it represents the number "1" standing for the beginning, "0" which stands for nothing or no-thing, and finally, number "8" standing for Infinity. That's why the Mala is so precious to use, as it connects you to a deeper meaning with the Universe. Also, having an object in hand mentally reinforces the ritual, just like f.ex. Lighting a candle, incense up to the use of a toothbrush as a little personal ritual in personal hygiene...All are tools that reinforce you and help you become more aware of what you are doing now. This is a personal choice for you and your very own ritual, as Rosary or Subha beads. The importance is really to hold something physical in your hands that has a connecting meaning to you; while you shift beads per beads you start your ritual. Mind yourself that you are not praying to any god; this is not something religious, but more of an Ode to yourself. Grateful for yourself, rewiring and reprograming your beliefs. And with gratitude, thanking your physical body for being alive and for all functioning perfectly. This morning is a new opportunity, a new chance, a new beginning to move forward and leave behind what has happened and remains unchanged and cannot be changed. All happens in the present moment as it can, with conscious awareness and attention, interfere and change your future. The fact that you woke up this morning and you are still alive is already the most beautiful gift in and of itself.

So, how does the ritual start? This starts early in the morning; while you wake up an hour earlier or half an hour, it is important that you prioritize yourself. I like to call this morning ritual the "Mala prayers" or you can also call it the "Gratitude prayer" which is done in 3 parts. This morning ritual will be part of your daily routine, just like when someone can't leave the house without taking a shower; you will come to a point where this personal well-being ritual cannot be ignored whether you are on holiday or not; it is going to be fully part of your life no matter what. This becomes a new habitual healthy routine, physically, mentally, and on the astral plane of your being. So, let's dive into how this starts...

As explained, this Mala prayer ritual is a three-part meditation done on a daily basis, early in the morning with your favorite brew, before you take a shower, and you go on with your day. The first part is all about being thankful for your three bodies (I.e., physical, astral, and spiritual). You are, in this first part, being thankful and grateful for how your physical body is functioning perfectly for you. We never think of this; no one does as it is so normal, but have you ever thought of how magical your biomechanical system is working? You are breathing naturally without even needing to think of it. While this inhalation of oxygen and exhalation of carbon dioxide is primordial for us to exist, obligate anaerobes and deep-sea ocean-level floor bacteria are harmed or even killed in the presence of oxygen. Isn't this engineering of life just marvelous? While you breathe, you bring life into your entire organism. Your entire inner community of 50 trillion cells takes what you give them and shares food and air, information to keep the entire system functioning and operational in a compassionate and infinitely loving way. A government; an ecosystem within that works with infinite love and compassion. There is no differentiation between each different cell or organ. The way how you eat and then process it all in digestion. A renewal of cycles between the wanted, needed, and the unwanted waste. It's just perfect engineering, and for that, we are grateful! So, let's start with the physical body, for which we are grateful for its five elements: earth, water, fire, air, space/ether. These elements are what make our physicality, the earth being our molecules, particles, the matter your physical body is made out of; water is found within your circulatory system in your body; fire is the heat you produce; your temperature is constantly regulated through homeostasis, the air is present in our system through breath intake and exchange, and finally space or ether is the capacity your physical body holds. Now, we move on to the astral body, which has nineteen elements in total. We start with the five first basics that each human normally has, and we are grateful for our five senses, which are our senses of touch, taste, smell, hearing, and sight. You might ask why sight is part of the astral body. Let's say you see and observe a flower. As you watch the colors, the forms, and the symmetry, you are fully immersed in the beauty of it.

Now, I want you to close your eyes and visualize a sunflower...Can you "see" the color yellow? The symmetry and geometry of the flow of its grainy textures are spiraling from the outside into the inside. The yellow petals on the borders overlap, long and large, with a silky texture. Now, open your eyes again. So, let me ask you if you saw the flower. You did, even if it was not physically in front of you. This exercise can be done with all of your other senses, and therefore, these are all part of our astral body and not on the physical plane. The next five elements of the astral body are those of the five actions of the physical body. We are grateful for the actions of the upper body (movements from waist to above), the actions of our lower body (movements from waist to below), the action of speech, the actions of the genitals, and the actions of our sphincters related to the digestive tract; located in our throat, at the beginning of the stomach to finally the anus sphincter. We never take the time to say thank you for all of that, right?

How grateful can you be that these sphincters open and close at the right moment? Having the anus sphincter constantly open would seriously be a physical problem. So, we are just grateful that this autonomic nervous system works perfectly well without our voluntary interaction. Next is now being grateful for our 5 energy levels, our vital forces out of yogic traditions such as Apan, Vyan, Saman, Pran and Udan. Apan, having the "earth element," relates to any physical matter such as excretion, sweat, and tears. Vyan, which holds the "element water," supports all circulation, transfer, and movement of water and other fluids in our body. Saman has the "element fire" and thus enables the energy used for digestion up to the built-up heat in a workout to flush toxins out.

Pran(a) (I.e. the numbing of "a" spelling will depend on the north or south of India). Pran holds the "element of air". Its vital energy is transmuted into the heart valve pump that transfers all nutrient blood flow through the entire system. The air that fills the lungs through breath is oxygen transferred to all vital organs and cells feeding them. That's also the reason that prana is called the life force energy. It keeps everything alive and in existence. It is no wonder that the first organ created in a developing fetus is the heart. The last of the 5 energy is Udan, which holds the element of space and operates on energy refill from above the heart direction head. Here is where all of the energy intake comes from. This intake of energy principally comes in the form of food and sun. There are still many forms of energy intake and recharge, but this will be explained deeper in the coming chapters. For Udan, energy fill comes from the food you eat or sunlight. You might have already noticed when u start to feel tired or get a headache, it's mostly because you need energy, which is our fuel to keep going on.

Either you eat something or drink a big glass of water and feel good again, or you go out in nature and take fresh air and get sunlight to recharge. After doing these actions, you are fit to continue and go on with your day. Depending on what you eat, this can also be energy-consuming and tiring, and instead of feeding and uplifting, you will feel lower than uplifting. Meaning this requires one to be mindful and conscious of what to eat. Either way, if you look at this, we are no different than a plant that needs a good, balanced, nourishing soil, nutrients to finally water, and sun or light to grow and survive. So, all is connected within the Universe, just on a different large scale.

Now, we are thankful and grateful for our four "inner instruments" that are still part of the astral body. These instruments are our mind, ego, intellect, and the subconscious. Let's start with the mind. What is the mind? In order to answer this question, you start thinking. The first thought is about the question of what the mind is, and further, down the road, another thought brings another one, and so on...to not go too deep into philosophical topics or the nature of the universe, I "think" we can all agree on a simple fact that the mind a bundle of thoughts is. Next is the ego. We will dive deeper into the ego and its fragmented nature in the next chapters. But to keep it simple, first, we will go into primarily understanding what the ego is and it's very basic function because this way of being grateful and thankful to this part of you in time will make you re-think how you want to respond. This part in you, this so-called ego, can be broken down into a main principal property of two things: the first being that the ego is the attachment to your ideas. This is the base part of a conversation that will turn into an argument. Because you have two separate ideas taking place in a position where each person is attached to what they think or believe to be true. The argument then explodes by the second nature of the ego, which is the identification of your thoughts (I.e. initial idea). The moment you get attached and then identify with your thoughts/ideas, you become the emotion of anger, etc. The ego is now active and kind of takes over you. You become possessed by the ego. Moving on to the next instrument, the intellect. Now, what is the intellect? This is what separates us from other animals. I don't want to generalize it too much because animals also have their instincts, their way of being and surviving. None of the less, only we, as human beings, have this capacity of intellect. In a sort of two-way sword, this is also what may hold humanity too confined in a box rather than reach a higher level of consciousness...but we will dive deeper into that too. Basically, the intellect is our capability to analyze and thus process information. But just as the mind limited is, knowledge can also just be ass limiting you. Finally, the last of the four inner instruments is the subconscious. For this, we will have chapter 10 to dive deep into the subject. Acknowledge this subconscious part is the first major step as you flash the light on a dark, forgotten, and suppressed corner in the psyche. The subconscious is part of your inner unconscious programming, the socialization that made you be you today, and this entire recollection of experiences that makes out your behaviors and thoughts and the personality you identify with as of this day.

Lastly, we give thanks to our spiritual body and its four elements, which are the soul, karma, free will, and samskara. The soul is the infinite essence in you that uses your physical body as its vehicle to experience the world around you. Karma is one of the laws of the universe that states that every action you do or put outwards has an equal or opposite reaction, which can also be observed in Newtonian physics. Free will is the fundamental law of the universe. That states that every being has free will. You always have the power to choose for yourself, no matter the situation. Take the example of someone being held against their will; no matter the traumatic experience, they still have free will over their thoughts, which no one can ever take away from them. Another scenario could be that you are being put through so much pressure that you decide to do what is requested or imposed, such as in manipulation, so you will be so pressured that you will choose to go their way even if this happened through a forced way this was still your choice based on your own free will. Lastly, samskara is your ability to consciously remember your past life experiences; this can also be understood as having access to the Akasha library, also called the Akashic records.

As an energetic being, you can meditate consciously, choose where you put your attention, and go on an inward journey. Many have then accessed astral travel to Samskara, where they could access information about past lives and any other realm where time-space reality no longer exists.

This first part of thanking our three bodies with all their elements is now done. To sum up, we have thanked our physical body, which has 5 elements, and our astral body, which has 19 elements. The spiritual body and its 4 elements. And each element thanked was one mala-bead continuously moved through your thumb and first finger.

Now, we close our prayers about the three bodies while all of this is still part of the first part of your mala ritual. Still, each thanks, acknowledgment, and awareness will be given by you moving your beads one by one. I will be talking in first person so you can really feel immersed in this closing part.

I'm grateful and aware of the mastery of my three bodies and my ability to let go of anything that is not under my control.

I'm grateful and aware of my duties, which I always do at my very best with no expectations and no attachments.

I'm grateful and aware of the maya. I may interact with the illusions around me, but I will not be affected by them, either attached or blinded.

I'm grateful and aware of the universe, that it is always working for me, in symbiosis, supporting me with its laws of actions and reactions. Its laws of gravity, to manifest and to magnetize the laws of attraction, also called laws of mirroring, to its seven laws of the universe correlating to the seven chakras, and finally to the laws of free will.

I'm grateful and aware of my mind and its bundle of thoughts. I always release the perfect positive, uplifting thoughts and, in doing so, release the needed chemical components and hormones within my pharmaceutical brain.

I'm grateful and aware of desires, pleasures, and materialism. I am aware that these states are all just temporary and are just being fulfilled by the gratification of my five senses.

I'm grateful and aware of happiness and sadness. I am aware that these states are also just temporary and are only fulfilled by my expectations at a given moment in time.

I'm grateful and aware of the only state of my mind that is permanent. The only state that balances the pendulum of the mind is the state of peace and equanimity. Now that the three bodies and the mind are all balanced in peace and equanimity, we give gratitude to each chakra, also called our energy centers. We thank them with our eyes closed and visualize each of them with their qualities and elements. The seven chakras are as follows: 1st Muladhara Chakra (located at the base of the spine), 2nd Svadhishthana Chakra (located three fingers below the navel). 3rd Manipura Chakra (solar plexus, navel region). 4th Anahata Chakra (heart space). 5th Vishuddha Chakra (throat space). 6th Agya Chakra (third eye, space between eyebrows) and finally, the 7th Sahastrara Chakra, located four fingers above your head, like a crown. We continue the thanks and gratitude in order from one to seven. I'm grateful for their elements of earth, water, fire, air, space, avyakta (I.e. gross matter & energy), and none (I.e. the seventh chakra has no element). Again, here, it is in order from one to seven. I'm grateful and aware of their qualities, which are grounding, collecting, birthing, and survival. I'm grateful and aware of desires, pleasures, materialism, and the reproductive organs. I'm grateful and aware for the dissolution of my ego, limiting beliefs and fears, and for the rise of my highest god/goddess self, for willpower, courage, strength, motivation, taking action, and having all the bravery in me; for the fire in me that heals all my internal organs and glands and the fire in me to thrive in life. I'm grateful and aware of the attachments that I have learned to let go of and that I only hold space for compassion and unconditional love. I'm grateful and aware for communication and speech that my words come from compassion, wisdom, and source, from a guiding and healing space rather than from a space of manipulation, ego, anger, and deceit. I'm grateful and aware of agya chakra that I see the world with the highest perspectives of my highest self; I see with my intuition, insight, true north, and inner compass rather than seeing the world with fear, biases, and filters covering the sight with the illusionary matrix. Lastly, I'm grateful and aware for Sahastrara chakra for my connectedness with the source energy of everything which I can interfere and interact with, for my kundalini shakti power to be fully aligned, that my Nadi Shodas of Ida (I.e., lunar/ feminine energy) and Pingala (I.e. solar/masculine energy) are both fully balanced in harmony, that I can access my metaphysical, magical, powerful, psychic abilities and that I can access astral travel, the akasha library and communication with beings, spirits, and ancestors of other densities.

I'm grateful and aware of the expansion of my consciousness and awareness, that I am able to be in the powerful now, the present moment, and that I have left all negativity about the past and future behind.

I'm grateful and aware of the peace and equanimity over my entire being, the harmony within my inner universe, and the entire universe at large. So, I wish well-being for all beings in all dimensions and densities.

<< *Namaste* >>

You see only within the first part of this mala prayer/gratitude prayer you feel revived and energized like almost untouchable to what is going to happen throughout the day. Also, being aware of your survival mechanism makes you start to think differently about how you will choose to react to any situation. You feel more grounded, balanced, and connected with your surroundings. How a perfect way of starting your day.

The second part is what I call the visual "Medicebo," which is done through visual meditation with a placebo effect on the brain and body.

You may have heard of how the placebo effect can be strongly effective on a person. They believe in taking the healing medicine in a trial, and suddenly, they heal or feel better even though they weren't given the real medication but a sugar pill. So, what happened here? It was the power of thought and belief. That belief was so strong that it physically affected them, even though it had started just by the thought of it. Thoughts are based on very, very high-frequency energy. And this can influence you positively or negatively, but we will dive into that further down in the book. But for now, it is important for you to understand that energy has the power to influence, change, and modify matter when your actions are applied with full awareness and consciously. This starts with you connecting to your heart. You start feeling vibrant high emotions and feelings such as gratitude, unconditional love, appreciation, and joy while keeping your attention to the heart space. Then, while you visualize the ailment or healing you want to create, while you deeply breathe in and out slowly and longer than usual, you imagine how all is aligning for you. As you breathe out, you are grateful as if all the healing had already happened. Note that manifestation works exactly in the same way. Believe that slowly, miracles will start to appear and happen for you.

Because what you want to heal in your body is very individual, I cannot give you guidelines, but the more you are precise in your "mental visualization," the more it gets effective. You can always find on the internet or in books what a cell or organ looks like and where its location is. Here is one example: with elevated positive emotion, you can visualize your liver and kidneys; as you slowly gradually breathe in, you imagine how they are cleansed, healed, regenerated, birth new cells, healing any eventual Epstein-Barr virus, cleansing any virus, bacteria, toxins, and heavy metals. Now as you slowly and longly exhale, and you physically feel how your body shrinks, you visualize like a stream of colorful water how all goes down (I.e. any unwanted matter & energy) direction poo and pee.

#

The last and third part of the Mala prayer ritual is your very own re-programming of who you want to become as a new person and what you want to change in your behaviors in order for you to move on and become the best version of yourself. Where do you repeat unwanted behaviors? Are you experiencing shame, limiting beliefs, frustration, or anger? We will understand this deeply in chapter 10. Notice just that in this last part of your ritual, as you talk to yourself, shift bead per bead, and change how you think or feel, you are re-writing old unwanted programming that no longer serves the "You" you've become today. As you repeatedly do this daily, slowly, it becomes a habit, and the way you think and feel about yourself then becomes an automatic behavior that transforms you into your new personality.

#

Chapter Two

Contemplation and the importance of deconstruction

#

You are now walking the path of change, the spiritual path, also called the path toward awakening. This shift happens in you the more and more you realize you can't go on with the unwanted patterns or situations that you have to deal with over and over again in your life. Either this happens by your own recognition or energetically, your body will manifest physical ailments in order for you to stop neglecting parts of you or suppressing emotions away by ignoring them. This is where contemplation through deconstruction of the mind, ego and beliefs becomes a very important first step in your inner work. If you think back, all the knowledge you know today can all be retraced back into your past. The way you had to be socialized in order to be accepted into your "tribe", society or the family, to the system you grew up in. You learned

31

and where provided things, acknowledged patterns, and had care and support up to the way how you "should" behave. This process happens through your parents, caregiver, school, society, culture, religion, politics, academia...the list goes on. All of that has contributed to shaping who you are today. Now, I want you to think back with all this knowledge you have, this "programming" you have received, how do you navigate in life? Does everything come easy and effortlessly to you? Do you still resonate with that today, or do you struggle? One thing for sure is today, you are no longer the same person as you were in your teens, and still you operate from those old beliefs that might not be serving you anymore. You can look at this like a computer operating from old software. Everything goes very slowly and very difficult because it desperately needs an update, and the old programs no longer support the newer version. Let us dive deeper into how we can change this old program and discover your very own truth for yourself.

Deconstruction always starts with questioning. Questioning all you have ever learned and all that has ever been told to you. In doing so, you will find answers for yourself, no matter how it ends, if you can give your very own final point of view on the subject or if the subject remains unanswered; the way you used to view that topic has changed. The importance of this is that you can see things differently from your own point of view and not from the point of view of someone else. How does this start? Well, first of all, set yourself a timer because your mind will want to wander in the first 10 minutes. At best is to set a half an hour per subject. At best, you will want to deconstruct one subject at a time. There are many things you can deconstruct, such as what a belief is. Or what is a thought? What is judgment, culture, reality, duality...to what is an object? Or the hardest ones: what is god, or who am I? This might sound strange, but this is highly beneficial for the expansion of your consciousness as well as for building new neural pathways in your brain. You can pick any subject that you were confronted with in childhood; if, for example, you grew up in a very religious environment, you can then deconstruct what religion is. Such exercises like these can be highly beneficial to heal and open your eyes or rather your "mind" at best. After you have set your time frame and picked one subject (I.e., always one at a time), you will, at best, want to write it on paper or in a notebook. Stay away from phones, notepads or computers, as these might distract you with ads and emails. Also, writing by hand on paper with a pen creates an intimate moment just for you. Like a personal ritual, you reconnect with yourself undisturbed. Let's try an example together: what is value? Sit with this one subject. Think deeply for yourself. The only source of "research" allowed is within your own mind, meaning your very own direct experience. Anything you ever learned from others, such as teachers, family, friends, school, academia, books, culture, science, religion, politics, none of these external sources are allowed. Even tv, newspapers or Google cannot be used. You need to deconstruct this subject as if you were a child discovering and analyzing "what is value" for the very first time and only as said in your direct experience and absolutely no other external source. Mind that your ego will want to take you to the answer like you already know that...don't fall for that trap. Your ego doesn't like this work as you might dissolve it during the process, ass you slowly detach from the known and start discovering all for yourself. If you start to feel confused or kind of lost, alone in the world with that question in mind, you are on the correct path of deconstructing!

Here is an example of you only using your direct experience to answer the question: what is value? As I start searching in my direct experience,

I think of value; what is that? Ok, I value my mala necklace; it is important to me, and I relate to it as a very powerful personal ritual for growth, healing and mindfulness. However, another person might see that necklace as just a piece of jewelry, as if "value" could be important to someone while, for someone else, it is unimportant. Could it be that value relative is? But what decides what is relative or not? Maybe the fact of seeing something from a different perspective gives it a sense of importance. Slowly, I come to think, that value is relative and that its importance is only measured by the perspective of the observer relating to it. Seen or thought this way, could I say that value has its very own energy?

I think I came to a conclusion that truly resonates with me. Value is an energetic perspective.

I hope now you can start to see where I'm trying to bring you with this technique.

You see, no matter how I thought before of what value was all about, what people told me about it, up to even now when I check it out on the internet (I.e., of course only after discovering for myself) the meaning of value has completely shifted and changed for me. I have a different understanding of it, and I made up my mind about this just by myself and not by what others might say, such as value, meaning money or importance. I created my very own understanding. This is why deconstruction plays a major role in your inner work; you start to discover your own truth instead of just blindly following others. You are no longer just like a kid who sits at the table and eats the cake, but you go deeper. You want to know the ingredients of the cake; you want to know how it is made from consumer to creator and how you perceive Reality today as it is, today as the adult you are. This way, you can now go back into your childhood memories and experiences, search deep into what was always told to you, what rules you had to comply with and follow, what laws you had to obey, what boundaries you were confronted with, and slowly step by step you pick your subject and deconstruct it. No matter the outcome of what you deconstruct, either way, your vision will have shifted, and what you were always told will no longer be valid. While we are diving into this deep inner work, let's dive deeper into your subconscious part of the brain. Again, for this, you will need to set a time frame for yourself, a pen and paper, or a notebook. At best, you can set a time frame of sixty minutes and choose a quiet space where you know you can work undisturbed just by yourself. Notice that you are in a safe space, no one can see you, and the work you will do now will be very personal. No one needs to know or see what you will write down. What will be revealed will not only change your perspective but deeply affect your ego. To some degree, parts of the ego might even dissolve because this confrontation gets into its core of attachment, and the mirror reflection will be too much to keep the "old" image up.

On your silent chosen space, take your pen and paper; as a title on your top page, you write down: "here is my judgment list I have done to others in the past". Write all the judgments you made around you, moments as you observed people or situations, simultaneously having your own self-talk conversations in your head while at the same time smiling back at them or quickly looking away. I want you to write all the positive, but also all the negative aspects you have ever judged on others. For this entire time frame that you've set up, you will go deep writing it all down. No one is watching; it's alright. Start now...

When you are done with your judgment list on others, you can take that page and put it aside for now.

Then, for the second part of the exercise, take a second paper or notebook; here again, you will write the title on the top of your blank page: "here is my judgment list I have done to myself in the past". The same principles apply here with a set timer. You retrospect, dive deep within, and start writing everything down. All of your positive self-talk but also all of your negative self-talk, your judgments and actions on yourself, the good, the bad, positive and negative, your inner critic when you observe yourself in the mirror or even the situations you have dealt with in the past. Anything that pops out write it all down. Again, this is an intimate practice, and no one is watching or judging; pour yourself out on paper.

When you are done, take some time to breathe and give yourself a break. Go outside in the fresh air or sun. You did some deep work here, and this is challenging and painful. But the bravery you are putting into doing this work will come with some very big payoff.

I want you to now go back to these lists you wrote down and compare them. Your judgment list on others with your self-judgment list. Can you find similarities? Do you find crossing situations? The very thing you have judged on others came back into your own list. Being aware of this written truth is your very first step towards healing. What is right in front of you can no longer be unseen. When you judge others, these are only deep hidden aspects of how you feel about yourself. This is where all roots of shame have also started because everything comes back to a process of repeated cycles. To understand this, all you need to do is go back into your childhood and think about any judgment that was made to you. Now you can start to understand that all has been functioning in projection; the shame and fear projected towards you by adults as you were young were their very own shame and fear. So, the shame and fear you experienced were never yours to begin with. Yet, as you picked that judgment up, you simply accepted that as a truth because that was your only way of being accepted or loved. But the reality now, as you see it, is that you are doing the exact same thing around you. Can you now still go on judging others? Knowing you might be just judging parts of yourself again at the same time unconsciously?

One of the fundamental laws of our Universe is based on the laws of mirroring, attraction and gravity. Your thoughts (in chapter 9, we will dive deeper into thoughts itself), actions and reactions are just at the end, an energetic signal or vibration you are sending outwards. The hearings of what goes around comes around are based on these phenomena others have experienced before you. Some call it Karma, but in the end, all can be seen as repeated cycles or, simply put, the wheel of life. What you put outwards is frequency and energy; by the very laws, you then can only become a vibrational match for what you think or feel. Isn't it a mystery to see that when negative, unwanted or bad things happen and you're only focused on that reality, the worse it gets, the more problems come one after the other? One might feel showered with a strain of bad luck. Or take it the other way around: one good thing and positive situation happen one after the other, all just good vibes; one might say they are showered with a strain of good luck.

The saying that you create your own reality is not so far-fetched. But let's take it slowly and step by step. It's not as easy as it sounds. Further down this book, we will dive into programing and the subconscious mind in detail. But for now, you are willing to change, and you are willing to heal. This started with you doing the mala prayers daily and doing the inner work. It's important for you to realize how your mind works and your ego's state of attachment identifications and beliefs. This work of deconstruction, questioning, diving inwards and retrospection is the way to start. For this, you need to acknowledge the judgments you made on yourself and how you see the world around you. The filters and biases you obtained since you were a child need to be completely stripped off so you can start from zero. Just like the saying of tabula rasa (I.e., "Blank slate"), discovering who you really are by yourself and not by how someone else told you it was the appropriate way to behave or act. For this work, any thoughts, feelings and emotions need to be fully acknowledged. Suppressing these will only make it come boomerang back to you. The process of deconstruction goes hand in hand with integration. Ask yourself why you feel the way you feel. When a problem arises, instead of asking why is this happening to me, start reversing the question by asking how is this happening for me. What can I learn out of this situation? What can I learn by experiencing this problem or challenge? You start seeing the world around you with a different perspective, a different lens. The lens you have chosen to look through. You see, you cannot just say to someone you create your own reality; this might apply to higher dimensional perspectives of the ultimate Truth, but not for now, not for someone starting the journey towards spirituality or simply ending one's sufferings. It needs to be approached

41

one step at a time, like stairs you start to walk up slowly. Starting at the lowest level and moving up higher. Everybody is in their own time, state and level of consciousness and awareness. It's like an onion that is being peeled off layer by layer until we get to the ground core of who we really are at the fundamental basic truth. You are a human being struggling, fighting and wanting to be the best version of yourself because this pain is becoming unbearable. If not, you would not have chosen to start reading this book or researching healing techniques to change your life. But this entire process doesn't happen overnight but intensively through deep work within your psyche and your mind, up to the very understanding of how you want to perceive your reality. The struggle, the trauma, the drama from the past made who you are and what you are striving for today. Still, it is your choice of free will to start doing the inner work to change.

And that is why I want to talk about resistance. Resistance is the very, very base foundation holding you back. The very reason of its existence is because during all these years of your lifetime, resistance has been protecting you. It is the very existing nature of your fear and of your ego. Fear can be spelled as a fragmented ego-attached reaction. The ego is nothing but your attachments and identification to your image, programming and sense of materialism. It has its purpose in your life; because the struggle, the trauma, and the abandonment, it was necessary for you to create it all in your psyche as a protector in order for you to survive. In order for you to meet your needs, when no one was doing that for you. Take a look at this example to understand one of the protector parts that enabled you to survive in your childhood or teenage years. Let's say that you were crying because you needed attention, you needed help, you needed someone to understand your pain. Yet mom or dad or any caregiver told you to keep quiet and act properly, that this emotion is unaccepted, and that you need to stop right now and behave. What did this tell you innerly? Showing your emotions is not ok; showing your feelings is not ok. It means you are rejected and not accepted in society. In order to survive in that time and space, you created the part in you, the protector that said to keep all your emotions inside, or else you will be alone. Today, you might never show how you truly feel, and this is messing up your life. It's messing up your relationships, your work life, and your personality, telling mixed-up messages in your head.

Beware that this is just one protector part inside you; you have many, many more that you are unaware of. Parts and fragments that might have served your very survival but that are no longer needed today. But we will dive deeper into that further down the road, understanding what is holding you back, what is that protector part you no longer need. When people talk about ego, it's always said it's bad, and it needs to die. I see that as pushing something away from you. If you go back to our example, it served you. It had its purpose to keep you safe. So, don't reject it today. Your ego might come from very deep anger, frustration and fear, and it has many levels of power. From the explosive volcano that wants you to always be right and everyone is wrong. Or the ego part that is very vulnerable, making many talks and conversations in your head, putting you down, judging yourself, and making you feel like you are nothing, worthless, and not good enough. These are all aspects of fragmentation or the ego inside you. That is the very reason why this work of deconstructing all of your beliefs and mind is so important. Because for the very first time, you are confronting your pain, your aspects you have pushed away. And this is scary as hell, as this is shaking your foundation of protection that has kept you safe for so long.

So be mindful and know that it is ok to feel this resistance to do the work. This resistance you might feel in doing or wanting to start your mala rituals and work of deconstruction and questioning. If you're first thought is that this work is nonsense and not useful, you are resisting, and this is proof that you are touching something deep inside. Look at what happens when you suddenly feel attacked or aggressed by words or actions of others; a trigger happens, and suddenly you feel exposed and the immediate response or action from your side is going to rise up due to this trigger. This very work is the basis of understanding why this anger is rising. Why am I getting triggered? It all starts with questioning. Only by questioning your beliefs, thoughts and opinions can show you how to find answers within your hidden psyche. And so, the very work starts here by you ripping all of the ancient weeds out of the soil, including the roots. So, in this soil, you can now start planting new seeds. New seeds of your own. Creating this beautiful inner garden, harnessing all the powers within you. In doing so, slowly, not only do you become the new version of yourself, but in the process, you become the new person you truly are in your heart and soul. In time, as you have deconstructed all of your beliefs, ideologies, biases and filters covering your eyes, you will start to see the world differently. From the eyes of your highest perspective, from looking at the world around you with your inner compass and true north instead of having a cross-wired compass inside you.

Interaction with the outer world and the outer environment will become less challenging. Judgmental aspects will have dissipated as slowly your ego is being dissolved by acceptance of why it was even there in the first place. You cannot longer judge someone else without thinking you are doing that to yourself. You cannot longer be reactive to others without wanting to question: why am I triggered, or what is this trying to tell me or show me? You become more understanding of yourself, more gratitude, self-love, compassion and acceptance for what is happening around you. And believe me, this is a very game-changer. It might be scary and uncomfortable, but only because you are now willing to change. And mind that it is okay if others do not want to change; as I said, everyone is on their level of consciousness and awareness. But where you feel uncomfortable and where you feel resistance, there lies the very power towards your growth and healing. One cannot stay stuck in avoidance or comfort zone without after wards being challenged by the Universe at large. If you stay in your comfort zone, slowly situations will happen such as the death of an animal or close friend, or people leaving you, the strain of bad luck...these are all just signals that something is not right, something is not going towards the direction of expansion, and in return, you feel the effects of it. If you do not want to change, accept what is not right for you; if you blindly suppress or ignore what you truly want in your life, then reality will force you to do so. This forced reality can come as pain in the body or sickness up to depression. That will be life shouting at you to put the brakes on, take a pause and look within. Take care of yourself and be mindful because anything you put outwards, as said, will boomerang inward. As much as this work of introspection and questioning is hard, challenging and scary, it is your road to start healing.

Do this work slowly. Take your time on the weekends or at least when you are confronted with situations that make you cringe and want to react negatively. Start asking questions and deconstruct all of your beliefs and biases. Each time the subject has been deconstructed, it will be a new way of your own thinking rather than some other parts in you. If you are challenged by someone you think is evil, then simply ask yourself what evil is. Deconstruct that subject. You might find a deeper understanding of that person or situation. Maybe evil is not what you have been told about, good or bad. Black or white. Maybe there are nuances here that are yet to be fully understood. But if you do this correctly, question it just based on your own direct experience. Maybe the next time you are standing in front of this same situation you called evil, you might feel a deeper understanding of what is going on. Evil might just be the aspect of an abandoned child. So, the remaining question will be; are you going to be the one abandoning that child again? Or does the cycle end now with a new change? A new perspective on this life, a new view about problems you thought being unsolvable. A new vision out of your highest perspective. When you no longer see with the filters of biases and old beliefs you start seeing with your third eye.

#

Chapter Three

Journaling, Presence and Being...

#

Journaling, presence and being are the topics we will dive deep into in this 3rd chapter. One might ask why journaling is important. We see and hear this all around, but what is the nature of this, and how can this tool be of service to one's own personal growth and healing journey? Journaling can be seen as an important tool to use for you to process information and experiences. Life is here, your teacher, what you experience, how you act or react to situations; is in every experience a gift you can use to journal about it. Do you encounter situations or experiences over and over again where you wish you would have reacted differently about it? Where you think about what you should have said or done? Like if you were operating out of a subconscious program yet not knowing how to shift or change that? But you do recognize the pattern of what you don't want; well, that's where you can start. This is where journaling can help you process and understand. To do this, you first need to find the subject about what you want to journal about. The struggle or acknowledgment of something in your life, something you saw or experienced for yourself.

Again, here, you want to be away from technologies such as cell phones, iPads, computers, etc. Get yourself a beautiful journal where you can write inside with a pen. This creates an intimate moment, almost like a sacred ritual, just you and your thoughts...

Let's say you always need to have a clean house, but your partner is more of a relaxed person who will do the dishes later rather than right away. This drives you crazy as you want it all done immediately. And so often, you will do everything right away, and conflicts again and again rise out of this situation. You can use this example to go inward and maybe find a journaling prompt that says: "Why does everything always need to be done right away"? By yourself, relaxed in a quiet space, you start to go inward and journal about this. You might find that as a child you also needed to obey rules, and this made you never in control of what you really wanted to do. As a result, you grew into an adult wanting everything in control. All needed to be perfect as you want it, and now others needed to obey your rules.

In conclusion, at the end of your journaling, you might realize it's okay to let go of control. It's okay to be able to leave the mess for a bit and to trust that your partner will do what you have asked. Even if not immediately, you start to find some trust and relief in other people than just all on your shoulders right now. And so now, this control you had, you might see it differently. You can start doing things immediately without a fight or asking others because it's bothering only you and no one else. Also, you can ask for help knowing that it can be done later and must not be done right now.

Any situation you experience can be put in a journal. Any pattern you want to understand, shift, or change in your life that is constantly creating conflict or annoying you can be put in written words. All you need to do is find out what that is; what happened again that made you say I should have done this or that; I should have said this or that... When something happens right in the moment, it's too late, and what happened has happened. But when you are alone you can reflect back on the day or the situation. You can go back and process quietly and start journaling about that moment. You see, our brains can be seen as computers that process information, but when software no longer supports the system, the computer needs an update. So instead of repeating your same unwanted behaviors, you simply start to journal about it, and slowly you are realizing and finding out what is working for you. You went deeper, and again, you understand yourself more, you get to know yourself and your own psyche a little better instead of being in this repeating loop.

Now, what do you do with this piece of information? Writing once about this will not change any patterns or behaviors. But it's a start, the recognition and understanding of your pattern.

Psychological studies in the 1960's talk about how re-programing your mind, like thoughts or behaviors became a new anchored and engraved program in the brain after 21 days of consecutive repetition. This was seemingly first coined by Dr Maxwell Maltz, but since studies and research have been done about this, it has become the 21-day rule. So, we can benefit from this knowledge not only with our mala ritual for gratitude and pattern change but also for what you may have discovered for yourself in your journaling prompt. You can take that page and read it consecutively for 21 days, either in the morning or evening. Just try this out and watch for yourself; either way, what do you have to lose? Except for a bit of time and trial? You can only gain more power if this does work out for you. And it will; all is just a manner of willpower and the hard work and effort you put in yourself, and that is definitely not for nothing, nor a wasted time.

So next time you encounter new situations in your life, even the beauty you might see around, journal about it. Journaling is not just about wanting to change unwanted behaviors but also about being aware of the beauty that surrounds us. I found gratitude in a journaling prompt as I compared the biomechanics of a human vision compared to technologies. As I tried to capture with a camera the wonderful scenery I was experiencing as I watched a reflection on the sea on an evening night. There was a glowing, glittery movement. After research, I found what I was observing was noctiluca scintillans (I.e. sea sparkle). The point is that I was in wonder how my eyes were adapting instantly and so quickly to the dark, the lights, and the reactivity of my eye's retina.

My camera could just not keep up. Any image I took was nothing like what I was observing in the present moment. I understood that my camera could have kept up, but for that, I would have needed to switch gears, objectives tripods, etc... just amazing how the human eye works instantly without the need to change gears! This simply just made me realize to put the camera down and just observe and know that this image will just be kept in my mind. Some beauties we observe, we never take the time to truly be grateful for what we experience. Even the food on a plate or new places we visit. All need to be taken in a photo, phone posted on social media... I mean, there's nothing bad or judgmental about that. But sometimes, we just need to appreciate what we see with our eyes and keep this image in our memories where no one can access or see it. No one can steal or delete what you saw or experienced. And this is something magical to experience, this is what came out of my journaling prompt. That we can find gratitude for our sight in this present moment and experience, and no technology can be compared to your vision, such as in that moment I had experienced that I want to leave you with this thought about journaling, use it as your tool, to grow, to experience but also to heal and change.

This experience now takes us to being present. Presence in anything that we do in life. Rarely we think of being present in what we are doing because we are so focused on what we want to do later. Life is an experience that is always happening in the present moment. But our psyche has been habituated for so long and is perpetually searching for the next best thing that we have lost touch with the reality of the present moment. Haven't you realized this, that when you desire something, and then you get it, you are already looking for the next step? In the meantime, while you are running to achieve that future desire, you have been completely missing out on the present moment. All you do is then nothing but a means to an end. Life then goes so quickly by, that you wonder where did the day go? How did this week pass so quickly, up to months, then years where you wonder where time flew? Yet still, we strive for the future or reminisce about the past, not noticing that we are doing that in the present moment. When you think about your past, you revive your pain, your regrets, and your past actions into your present thinking. What actually has past was done, was over. Still, in the now moment, you think about it and bring all of your sufferings back alive. This is why the ending of a relationship is so painful because before you move on and go through the acceptance of the break up you revive it daily in your present moment. This is like experiencing the breakup over and over again. The grief, suffering, and pain over and over again. This is no different about the future; you wish, think, and dream about some place, experience, object, or vision. But when that future desire realizes itself, materializes itself that will yet again happen in your present moment. And so, if you deeply think about this; nothing ever really happens outside of the "now" moment. Then why not make that precious? It is actually in the present time where life truly really happens; that's why the present moment is something you hear so often in spiritual circles. Being in that now. This state is the only real one you can experience. Therefore, it is so meaningful and precious. Even time seems to be in a state of inexistence, a flow of unmeasurable observance up to its illusionary appearance. Have you ever noticed that when you are having so much fun, time seems to be passing by in the blink of an eye? As if enjoying each moment delightfully makes time run so fast. Now, let's say that you are waiting on a date that seems to be late. Have you again observed that every minute that passes seems like hours and hours of waiting, as your focus is placed on the "when will they be here". Your focus is on the future, expecting the person to finally arrive instead of being in the present moment. What about when you are in a hurry? Again, here the focus goes into the future, such as "I need to be there;

I'm already late". Strangely, all of the red lights on the streets are lighting up for you. Cars drive so slow in front of you, and the more you are getting triggered, annoyed, and stressed out of already being late, and now you need to deal with these slow drivers and constant red lights. The more quickly time passes, the more you are late to arrive. The more you enjoy, time flies, and the more you are present, time seems to cease to exist. You are present, looking at this wonderful person. The auric vibe and energy are so magnetizing, and now time stopped. All of these examples appear to show us variable states of time wherever you are concentrated and focused on the past, present, or future. Time starts to get relative when observed in the present moment. And the famous quote of James Redfield from the 90s explains this in a nutshell; "where attention goes, energy flows". Since then re-quoted and stated by many. This means really that if your attention goes into being fully present, you are in total control of not only time, but your life and decisions. This practice can be done as a conscious way of reconnecting with what really is, with our reality. In doing so, unlock many hidden potentials, magical insight, and information you can only perceive in the very present moment of being fully present in it. Take this basic, mundane example:

As you wash your hands, you feel the water running through your fingers, you feel the soapy creamy texture creating tiny bubbles, and you smell the fragrance of flowers, honey, and macadamia nuts as you rub your hands, palms, fingers, and nails. Suddenly, your random hand washing just turned into a three-minute meditative mindfulness in the now. And this is just one small example of many you can do. Don't let your life just pass by, but be totally aware and present, and you will find joy, peace, and little meditative practices to incorporate in your daily basis, each minute or hour up to the next thing you need to do. This attention you start to give to everything arising in the now is the doorway to truly enjoying all of what you do instead of using it as said to just be a means to an end. Our best examples in life of being fully present and aware of the now are babies, children, to animals. When you look at a baby, how joyful, peaceful, and attentional they are. They really just cry or laugh when they need something now, may it be food, care, and affection, or the need to be changed. They are so fully present; all that matters to them is the now to be taken care of. Children are the same. They play, sing, cry, and also ask for attention and care in the moment of the "now". They live a life of simplicity and mostly are wrongly understood because adults talk about later, or not now...wait...or be quiet. This turns the situation into a tantrum when, really, we could learn from them and the simplicity of appreciating the wants and needs that occur in the present. This finally brings us to animals; their eyes are truly just the portals of the rising desire in the present. A dog can look at you and ask for a walk, food, or playtime, and nothing to them matters other than that moment of now that you pick up the leash, food, or ball. They can also look intensely into your eyes and show their love and affection for you, and this doesn't matter whether you have a good job, a nice house, or big cars. They just love you for you, for who you are right now, granting them your attention in the present moment with a gentle stroke on their backs. We can all start by looking and observing around us how everything interacts and is interconnected. With this thought, we never want to be off-guard again; we want to appreciate the simplicity and beauty life can offer each second and minute of the waking day and start to see how mystical moments appear for us as we interact with the infinite field of consciousness. This is just the beginning of a small spiritual practice, but a massive return in manifesting your dreams and opportunities in the now, which you would never have been aware of if you had not paused to appreciate and look around you.

This brings us to our final closure of this chapter by the act of being. Here, I would like to quote William Shakespeare's Hamlet play: "To be or not to be, that is the question". This play was written around 1599 and 1601. Originally a contemplation of death and suicide by Hamlet. I would like to take this question from a different perspective of being. What does it mean to truly be? Or as asked to be or not to be. You are, therefore, you exist. But as humans, we have such complex brains and ways of thinking, behaving, past experiences, and triggers that result in a state of explosive actions and reactions. For me, in that moment, you have exploded; you become your ego; you become your anger; you became the fear, and so you no longer are. But how can we then "be" rather this unwanted reactivity? Each experience is different; each situation is different; each person you will interact with is different. But there is a way that you can step into more being. It's a technique that requires a three-perspective view. This will need practice in each situation or interaction with someone, but the more you do this, the more it will be easier for you. Life in and of itself will be your ground to practice. That's what's beautiful about being alive is that each moment, at work, leisure, or anyplace, anytime, life is going to be your teacher and your practice ground. The first perspective is the given situation, the setting, the conversation with the person, the spoken words, and the environment. The second perspective is your mind, your bundle of thoughts, your vision, and your interpretation of what you see and feel, all being processed in your mind as you are watching or listening, as emotions start to arise. The third perspective is being the observer as if you were having an out-of-body experience and you were watching the entire situation like a bird flying above the situation. This last state of being in the third perspective cannot at the same time enable you to be in your mind. This means that instead of being immersed in your rising emotions, you rather are observing them, and these two states cannot happen simultaneously. If you can apply this really daily into any interaction you literally can avoid conflicts, up to eliminate ninety percent of conflicts in your life. Because when you really think about conflicts, it's only one person being attached to their ideology, thoughts, and past experiences, and they want to cling strongly to their mind. But as said, if you are the observer, you are fully detached of that pattern behavior. In time, with this practice of observing first before preparing your mental reply, you might catch yourself thinking how differently you would have reacted before. The anchoring point for being is firstly to deep very deeply, bring presence into the situation. Listen mindfully to your situation or interaction. Ask yourself the following questions: why am I getting triggered by this? What is this anger or rising emotion in me? You can then later use these questions to journal deeply about it. But notice that while you are questioning your mind you are not at the same time reactive. In each interaction where there is conflict or arguments, it's because each person holds on to their ego; either they are in a state of power (I.e., I'm right, you're wrong, I know, you don't) or they are in a state of emotional baggage (I.e., this hurts I need to protect myself, my position). Any of these two states of power ego or baggage ego are volcano states. This volcano state is very explosive; any person in a volcano state you cannot express your state of position, nor can you calm them down. Anything that you would say, even in a kind way would come in a wrongful understanding. It's like fueling fire by fire. So, the only way here to interact with a volcano state is really to bring full presence and being. By your calm energy of listening, giving them space to explode, and holding space for just presence, you are energetically shifting the vibration in the room. We will dive deeper in further chapters about energy and frequencies, but for now you can acknowledge this primary state. In this state of calmness, compassion, understanding, and being, your energy is in a higher state of vibration. The other person in that volcano state as a counterpart is in a lower state of vibration. This means in that same room, you will have two types of energies, the higher vibration, and the lower vibration, and these cannot co-exist in the same room because they are not a vibrational match to each other. What will happen? Either the volcano will say: so, are you just going to stay silent? You have nothing to say? Then, because of your non-reactivity, they will storm out of the room. Either they will find another volcano to interact with, or when their energy has shifted they will come back to the same room with sadness or disappointment rather than anger and aggression, then the resolution can start. The other scenario would be that your high state of vibration of calmness, receptivity, and attention will emit the frequency outward to the volcano. That might slowly calm them down and lower the state of anger into the state of sadness or disappointment; either way, their initial start point of energy will shift to come close to yours or to adjust yours. As said, you can only stay in the same room with matching energies. To summarize this, each person, each situation or conflict, always arises from their own level of consciousness. In this universe, everything evolves in its own state and level of consciousness. Everything evolves and expands in its own time. If you keep this in mind, you can always find compassion and understanding for what is happening to them or around you. They do not know better; all operate just with what they have and know and so it's no one's fault. All is just an evolvement in time. Everyone has their own cross or burden to carry. It is not up to you to carry their burden, but having the acknowledgment of each being in their own level of consciousness you can interact with awareness. This will be a great relief in your pain and suffering when you encounter similar situations. Being in a state of the observer, having the deeper wisdom and insight will make you see the world with a different perspective. You might be the light that will cast the darkness away. In a world of polarities, we can never be fully free of the contrast of good and bad, dark and light, war or love, love or fear, etc... but with this knowing, you can navigate the storms differently. You can use your inner compass to go with the flow, the stream of awareness. So, you can choose to navigate life in a way that you will less suffer, less be in this state of hate, resentment and not being offended. If conflict arise, because they still will arise, even if we would have a perfect utopian world state, we would know how to deal with these rising polarities. Polarities or also called contrast, are part of our third dimension; it's exactly what will give you the needed possibility for expansion, which is therefore inevitable and needed as long as you live here on earth. Ultimately with all this knowing, it is up to you to choose how you want to interact with the world around you, any given situation, what you observe, conflicts or just how you live your life in general. However, you apply the tools of journaling, to presence and being into your life; will set the tone of your happiness, joy and the ability to live in peace and equanimity. Nevertheless, we can all start to see differently with the inner knowing and wisdom that what we see is neither just black or white, but we can all start to look for the layers in between and see the grey tone.

#

Chapter Four
Frequencies, Energies and Matter.

#

Our earth is made out of matter, if you look at it from the macro scale it holds a perfect vessel for what inhibits it. There is a harmony and order functioning out of infinite love, coherence and harmony. Operating from the highest levels up to the lowest. From water, trees, plants giving life for insects and animals. All feeding, nourishing each other and transferring information back on full cycle and circle. The water on this planet is made out of seventy- two percent and the oxygen ratio of twenty-one percent; and the entire system works together perfectly in symbiosis. In our human body the water ratio and our inhaled oxygen is equally the same. We never think about this, but the way earth is functioning with its perfectly organized "government" our bodies work just the same way. One could say that you are not just one human, or one person; but you are actually a community of fifty trillion cells. When we think about how our inner biomechanics work, how we nourish ourselves; all the nutriments are assimilated where it needs to go or expelled out, each organ work and communicate together without any differentiation. The moment a cell needs to die, they do so, they sacrifice for the greater good of the human body to keep functioning and renewing. If this wouldn't happen, and a cell would go rogue and not self-destruct itself when it's needed that is called cancer. Death and birth of cells is what is keeping us alive, but death is always seen as negative, given that it is crucial and very important for survival it should be as much and as equally be appreciated as birth. We can now start to see how really, we are on a micro level similar to the Earth. When we now think about energy or frequency, again here we can find similarities. Earth emits its own magnetic field and equally we emit our very own torus field, our energy field. This brings us to be more connected and appreciate Earth and being part of this entire system. And it should be a wake-up call to acknowledge how we are deeply similar and connected. Up to this day we are absolutely not living in harmony here on Earth, especially since the Industrial Revolution that started around 1760. We kept on depleting the earth's natural resources, especially in fossil fuels, oil, and gas, from deforestation to mining to obtain lithium for batteries. The more civilization and technologies are evolving the more we are coming to uncharted territories with what might happen to us in the future. It seems all are concerned to go greener or have more conscious business, but as long as big corporations, industries benefit of these resources it is challenging to change that. Free energy or anti-gravity technology energy will be a taboo subject and life threatening to the survival of big corporations and in return it remains suppressed to the benefits of humanity at large. A thing for sure is we cannot continue to act as a parasites on earth, because again compared to human bodies, it will use its natural immune system to clean up the very threat acting against it. But there is a way to shift this behavior, mindset and new way of being more conscious and aware. This will not only benefit the planet at the greater good but humans joy, peace, happiness, well-being, and ability to thrive as well.

As said above each of us has an innate energy field that we emanate. Back on chapter one we talked about the fields healing properties by connecting with gratitude with the heart and visualization (I.e. the mind/brain). By creating this coherence, we can make this energy field larger and larger, which enables us to connect to higher realms of consciousness and access mystical abilities yet to be fully understood by science. On the previous chapter we talked about how these frequencies also affect other people, but what is this exactly and how does it work? The higher the frequency, the higher the vibration you emit or perceive. This frequency can be compared to an old radio station, where you have a button to search a specific station for music. When you found the station, frequency acts like a radio wave. Then the vibration will act by a weak or strong transmission. Just like the radio that gives you the sound of music or news, your energy is frequency and frequency carry information. Beware that the information here travels faster than the speed of light, so that it's literally an instant exchange of information. And this field you emanate is connected to all there is in existence. Some scientist calls this a unifying field, believed before it was a vacuum or empty space but this no longer makes sense. I like to see this field as the infinite source of Consciousness. In this source field even Newtonian laws no longer exist, even less the laws of causality and probability. In quantum mechanics, such as in the double split experiment, the probability of determination by the particles after trajectory could either have been a wave or matter, up until it has been observed. Observation is not only what brings an equation in the experiment, but consciousness (I.e. you) are part of the equation. Now you can start to understand how you are a primordial part of this equation, this mystery science cannot yet solve or understand; but how can we now relate about everything being connected? In science, quantum physics again here made some experiments called quantum entanglement, which Albert Einstein never really was fond of. What was happening here in the experiment is that information was traveling faster than the speed of light. Information was instantly shared, and that's when Einstein quoted this as a "spooky action at a distance". A single proton was split with a laser into two identical electrons separated at large distances. In this observation experiment an electron can display two different positions. Either a spin up or a spin down. However, as the experiment started and one electron's position was observed; when it had a spin up, instantly the other electron also had a spin up. The same way as the other was later observed with a spin down, instantly its half twin had the exact same position. Up to this day the furthest distance observed holds a record of

1,200km where the entanglement (I.e. instant showing same position) was observed.

This experiment shows us, that everything in this universe is connected with each other within this field of consciousness. If you look at the Big Bang theory or god creating everything. We can agree on all forms that all has started out of a point of singularity. If so just like in the experiments of entanglement, all coming from one source we all have this innate instant connection. We all have had this inner voice talking to us, this sudden insight or intuition. You think about someone and suddenly your phone is ringing and they are calling or either texting. But this goes even further than that sense. In military, c.i.a operations even made studies about telepathy which then was used for experimental trials. There is an innate inexplainable energy connecting us all with each other, the bond we feel with other humans, the bond we feel when we go out in nature, the bond we feel with animals. This connection is what is keeping us healthy, strong, joyful and also having a purpose in life. All of our experience on earth from positive ones up to negative ones are all linked to connection. Imagine in some part of your life you felt this feeling of shame, that you were not good enough. These are very powerful painful emotions, because this feeling is exactly in opposition of connection. Shame tells you that you don't belong to the tribe, society or either the norm of what says "normal" ...

Being in this inner bubble of rejection, where no one understands you, and worse of all even if you are surrounded by other people you will still feel alone and "not part of". We will see further in the subconscious chapter where and why this has started, but you need for now just to understand that we are surrounded by all energy in existence. You are part of something enormous, and when you start seeing your connection not only within your cells and body, but also within the entire world, the rest of the connection with other people will slowly fall into place. We are social species, just like wolf packs we are not made to be alone or left aside. That's where all depression anger, up to suicide can come from. But when you reconnect with yourself, with you desires, passion, dreams you are aligning yourself with the highest energies source. Ever wondered when you follow that inner voice, how it brings wonderful situations, new opportunities up to new people into your life? There is a powerful connection and the more we acknowledge this the more we start to understand its relations to us humans and our entire connection and purpose within the universe.

This energy is not only connecting us as previously explained but also has powerful healing properties. In Yoga, Qigong, Reiki, Crystal healing up to Quantum healing (I.e. comparable to the visual medicebo in chapter1) are all a few examples of the most important healing techniques that include movement with energy. The mala prayers, specially the second part we saw on chapter one is all about healing and moving the energies with intention as well as for the expansion of our torus (energy) field. Before traditional medicine was known, our ancestors only used the healing properties of energies and plants in order to treat sickness or energy blockages in their tribe. Today we have lost touch with the ancient knowledge, but I do believe all is slowly coming back full round circle to us. We see more of the energy healing traditions now emerging. Humanity is getting back in touch with what they have lost, especially in these past years where we have experienced suffering, manipulation, control and bulldozing. Slowly you are getting powerful and the more you access this inner power, intuition and wisdom the more you create balance and coherence in your life with what is truly essential and important to you. Ones one has realized this, nothing and no one can ever take their power away from them. No one gave you that inner essence, that inner energy is inside you, so beware that no one either can take that away from you. This energy, this source power inside was always available to you and always will be. This is a source fragment, within your soul, an essence that was never born and can never die. Infinite consciousness utilizing the human body vessel. Nowadays we often hear about manifestation. But was is that really all about? One might say this is some kind of woo-woo / new age stuff, but watch out and try it out for yourself. It's just like a game, where you finally understood how the rules work and how all operates and interacts with each other. You start to play a game where you can finally be the winner and make conscious decisions. And anyway, what do you have to lose? Except for again here some trial and time. Sometimes when all you have tried is just not working, be brave enough to step out of the comfort zone, break those prison and cages in your mind and try out some new things. Manifestation is exactly what it means to work with energies. When you are in a state of gratitude you're a vibrational match for the positivity, wishes and dreams you are imagining and feeling AS IF all has already happened. This way of acting and believing as if all has already happened by being grateful for it, is vibrationally creating an energetic pull towards you, as you are becoming an exact vibrational match for what you wish for. And that is what is called manifestation. This is like praying but in a different powerful and effective way. When you pray you basically just wish and ask for something to come. But when will it come? Also acting this way is sending the energetic vibe and intention that you are in lack. In this energy or lack, requesting and praying you are not a match for what you want. But more of a match to lack, unworthiness. And so, you keep on wishing and praying and never it happens... that's how powerful energy works with attraction, when you realized how it really works you can attract all your dreams, abundance, joy, happiness, health and wealth in your life. It is time for us humans to realize how much power lies in us, by starting to see what cannot be seen. Move away from physical reality and materialism and move closer by trusting the unseen, in that lies tremendous powers and gifts. Take a look at feelings, emotions, thoughts up to the wind, sun rays, radiations or Bluetooth waves; all of these exist but you cannot see it. All you can do is perceive the energy it carries. As said energy is a powerful carrier for information, what you express outward with intention has its message out to the universe, as all matter in existence is only pure energy. In the year of 1911th Ernest Rutherford, was the pioneer for studies of radioactivity. He was the first one to find out that an atom consists of mostly empty space (I.e. 99,9999999 %) and what makes out this empty space is pure energy. Our bodies made out of trillions of cells zoomed in, are purely made out of particles, protons, electrons, matter in the deepest level. We are multidimensional beings radiating energy. Looked at this way our bodies are constantly interacting with all these vibes, frequencies and energies at all levels. This is where also sensing inward grows the information you pick up outward. Have you ever entered a room or a space where you felt it had a welcoming, comforting good vibe? You felt cozy in this warm space, you felt at ease, at home. Same goes for a dark alley, or a room you entered and immediately you felt uncomfortable, not at ease nor at peace. You can feel something is off, something is not right. But this goes further than just sensing rooms or spaces. Your intuition, this insight we all innately have is what is connecting us with everything in existence. This bond is very very strong specially if you love someone or feel connected to others. A mother knows when something is wrong with their child, if they hide secrets or are in danger. A mother can sense this no matter the distance. Same goes for a close friend, you know even from a distance you suddenly think of them, when you text or call you find out they are in need of help and you reached out exactly at the perfect moment. The more you connect with this inner essence you get to live experiences and synchronicities in the universe that seem unexplainable and magical. You suddenly feel to quit your job, or to follow that inner voice, that then brings you to take the decision to go visit that place you always felt pulled to. Weirdly it is in that place that you meet amazing connections for a new business you always wanted to start by your own. Job opportunities fall onto your lap just like that, you seem to be at the perfect place at the perfect right time. All is aligning perfectly for you.

But for some humans they have lost touch and connection with this inner essence this infinite connecting energy field each of humans, animals and plants have. This comes purely from you suppressing that inner voice, that intuition inside by covering it and layering it by a made-up reality in your head to keep you safe. Your no longer live in the Reality but you have created one for yourself where you might never be hurt again, one where you will never be left alone again, one where you will never be shamed or abandoned. The more that voice, that inner energy is suppressed, the more it starts to get quiet. It is silenced by your own will for the sake of your protection. As you are thinking you are "protecting" yourself you are putting yourself and your loved ones in a very dangerous position. The universe based on these laws of energies and frequencies, expansion, attraction and free will, all this combined is always going to want to re-align you with your inner essence. But if this connection has been suppressed and silenced, the universe will do all it has in its powers to bring you back in alignment. This power of re-aligning will come in ways you cannot imagine, deepest hurtful ways in order to wake you up from your "imagined un-real reality". Death in this case, is the most painful lesson. The death of a closed loved one, is powerfully asking for you to see the pain, see and feel the grief. There is a call saying that life might be short, that you need to live life accordingly to what Reality is and needs to be lived in the way of what you really want to experience. Maybe also a call for saying you are living on borrowed time. Either way it is a deep call for a wake-up. Same goes for sickness or aches in your body, this is another call for a mental health healing and re-alignment of your Truth. Mostly when we live in this made-up reality in the mind, we take more than we can take. We accept more than we should, this all due to that suppression of the inner emotions, suppression and ignorance of the vibes and energies. This is then when things start to get blocked, or starts to get stagnant. Because the free flow of energy cannot be expressed in a totally free way. It is only when water is stagnant, that things start to rot, that life can no longer exist, bacteria, viruses and pollution on the rise in this stuck un-flowing water. That being said, these are all reminders of the universe calling for re-alignment and letting the energies in a flow of movement. Notice that when a person is starting to dive deeper in loneliness, in fear, they are left unacknowledged, ignored and not integrated. This person will be further and further apart from their inner essence, their infinite energy, their soul, their source consciousness. The more the gap and separation gets bigger and pulled apart; the only way for re-alignment in this case is the physical death of the human body. Think about what you have experienced up to this day; the most hurtful situations, in the very deepest and darkest pain, always have left you with a deep lesson or message learned. We need to start seeing that there is a gift in the negative as well as for the positive. In the end these are polarities that we can never escape from as long as we live this experience here on earth. And so, aligning with this energy, these highest frequencies we can start to use our power of healing and manifestation to start really living a life that is meaningful and purposeful. Following the road of energies, frequencies combined with the physical matter, is using all of the available the tools you have to experience life at its fullest. It is the merging of all of that, which enables perfect balance and equilibrium in source consciousness. The external reality that you will experience will mirror your inner universe within your body. Harmony found outside will reflect as the harmony found inside. Same as for stressors output outside affect stressors inside which we will see in the chapter about epigenetics in depth. When we start to understand how all Reality is reflecting upon each other's vibes and energies we no longer want to be ignorant and powerless. We want to create, let our inner alchemists out because that's what's happening when you realize that you are able to transform lead into gold. We just have to get back to our intuition. We have to listen closely again to that inner voice. Attune ourselves back into our vibes, the energies and frequencies inside. The more you listen again, the more all will come back. The more you start following your heart, feelings, thoughts and emotions, the more you are innerly waking up again. You are growing your inner energy field, you are sensing your Reality inward and reflecting it outward as it really is, and no longer in avoidance or coping mechanisms. This all truly starts by you listening inward, especially when time gets tough. Especially when you feel you are lost. The answer is inside you. Why do you feel, the way you feel? Instead of ignoring or avoiding go back to listening to that inner voice, that higher self. The more you will pay attention the more the silenced voice will rise again until you can clearly and loudly understand and hear it. That moment you will no longer can deny your Truth. Any problem will now be a treasure quest of what it is going to bring you. What is the gift in this stuckness or challenge. You are becoming energy and frequency, more than matter. And you are flowing in the streams of source, in a life guided by your heart and desire. Your expansion, as it benefits the Universe at large, will offer and mirror back exactly what you have dreamed of; a ride on a highway in the most unexplainable ways. The Universe will respond and sometimes will take you to the most unimaginable shortcut to what you wanted.

Finally, what I want you to takeaway about this entire chapter, is that you are powerful, beyond what humans think they are. In tremendous powerful ways, when you start to tap into that energy field inside you, when you learn how to navigate it inward and outward you are connected with the very highest form of Source Consciousness. And that's what lower state of vibration or lower state of consciousness people do not fully grasp. Suddenly they call what they saw or what happened a process of a sudden miracle. Since it cannot be "scientifically" understood and it's so mysterious it gets named mystical, magical, legends and tales, because they cannot find an explanation. But the explanation is you. The conscious observer, the conscious creator. As you follow your inner compass and meet slowly your powers you are stepping in to the mystical, spiritual dimension. The magician and alchemist that always has been existing inside you is waking up. You are accessing instant healing, regeneration of your cells, growth, repair, reconstruction and birth of new cells. You are tapping into your inner fountain of youth, reversing the myth of aging. Curing any disease that might have had that occurred in your unknowing state of negligence, you had put yourself through throughout the years. And those are only aspects in healing. When you are connected to this source field you expand your energy outwards, as you send information outward you start to take control of your life, what you want to create and attract back into your field of consciousness. If you can dream and imagine a certain reality in your mind, it means it can be created by you. When you become the vibrational match for what you have intended to; this Universe by its laws of this reality will have to mirrored it back to you. There is no other way around, when you start to consciously focus and create. Accessing other dimensions, astral travel, telepathy, higher states of consciousness, infinite source field of information are just a few to name to what you can access beyond healing. You are already all of that, the mystic is already you.

#

Chapter Five

Noble Gas and Relationships.

\#

A noble gas is an atom found in the periodic table of chemistry. Now one might ask what is the context of comparing a chemical atom with the way of human relationships in general? To answer this, we need to dive into the saying you might already have heard "As above, so below". Originally the entire quote says: "as above so below, as within so without, as the Universe so the Soul..." Quoted by Hermes Trismegistus (470 BC) author of various philosophical systems that are known as Hermeticism. One of the principles of these teachings is that all what you can analyze from a micro scale to a macro scale can be understood, applied and studied equally. From comparing small systems up to larger ones, and so in this case from atoms into humans; just as we have seen in the previous chapter as we compared earth and its similarities with our human biological system. The noble gases are a set of six atoms within the entire periodic table of one hundred eighteen atoms in total; and they act completely differently from the rest of all other atoms. These special atoms are Helium, Neon, Argon, Krypton, Xenon and Radon. What makes them so special is that they do not need to bind in chemical reactions. The fact of needing to bind into chemical reactions is actually to preserve energy due to their loss of energy alone. All other atoms wobble and lose energy; because they do not contain a balanced number of electrons or full number of electrons in their outer shell. That makes all of the other atoms an imbalanced atom, compared to the noble gases which are all balanced atoms on their own. In a nutshell all of the imbalanced atoms need to bind to other atoms in order to into be balanced and preserve energy. All of the noble gases with their full count of electrons in their outer shell, are all six of them independent balanced atoms. Now if we look at this closely we can recognize two patterns in this chemical world, meaning one of codependency and one of independence. When you look at human beings, this pattern can be observed as well. You got some people that need to bind themselves to others in order to feel whole. This is the type of codependent relationships that is really unhealthy. Because the fact of this codependent style of relationship, they are in a vulnerable space of insecurity and lack of trust. That's where all the questioning, and sneaking into one's phone or emails can begin. They are insecure, want to know where you are, what are you doing, who is texting... jealousy, anger and fear are on the rise. This can then turn into suffocating the other person up to creating conflicts and arguments due to this lack of trust and due to this constant need of being attached together. They cannot be alone, as if loneliness is a direct threat to their well-being. Same as that atom, that wobbles, and is not balanced on their own, these types of people cannot burden to be balanced alone. Alone they are just not whole, not balanced and feel lost. This type of relationship style can be retraced back to childhood, probably they were ignored, left aside, did not receive love and attention. They needed to be either seeking for constant attention which they never received, abandonment or either being a scapegoat or mediator in the family dynamic. This created adults that did not know how to cope when being alone and therefore meeting a new person means their entire world will turn and revolve around that person. Now if we go back into the chemistry atoms world, you might think ok, well I want to change my patterns become like a noble gas and be independent, whole and strong alone. Does this mean I will be alone forever? Actually, in chemistry when two noble gases meet they create laser lights! This means they absolutely do not need to bind, they are not codependent; however if they do decide to bind and pair with another noble gas, a different dimension of chemistry is created that comes into light. This means for the human way of looking at relationships; you can be strong, balanced and independent on your own. And when you are in this state of vibrational frequency the people you will attract will be the same matching properties. In such relationships you can together create laser light, have strong chemistry of love, trust and balance because the lack of trust and codependency doesn't exist. Both are strong alone, yet together even stronger. This is the kind of healthy way you want to live your life instead of being fully dependent on someone else. Patterns are hard to change at first but when you understand it, there is a way of overwriting the unwanted which we will dive deeper and see in the subconscious chapter.

This comparison of atom binding and humans binding, brings us to the understanding of connection, and this is the most important thing you can experience in this human lifetime. We absolutely are beings that needs community and connection, being excluded and alone is pushing one away that does not belong to the tribe. This literally means physical death in some tribes when one gets rejected or pushed away. Look at this example, when you experience a very painful breakup do you think of eating? Most of all, being deprived of connection is threatening your very own survival gene encoded in your DNA. I believe with this, that connection is even more important than food after water. What about society? Do you grow you own food? Do you live off-grid? We all depend on each other like it or not, the only question is at what level do you interact and how anchored are you in Reality. When we talk about relationships we usually hear things such as give and take. I do this for you, I sacrifice so you can be good and happy, and because of that we accept to have the same in return. Is that mostly happening? Not always...and mostly because something is going deeply wrong in this unhealthy dynamic. This is not the healthy way, when you need to sacrifice, cope and suffer then something is wrong and it should feel this way. There are two main ways of being in a relationship. This is valid, for romantic ones, family, business, any relationship dynamic. The two ways is the "poker face" game or the "showdown player - cards on table" game. The questions are which one are you playing? The poker face is when you are not truly honest nor with yourself, nor with the other person. You say things such as: yeah, it's fine, it's ok (while internally your entire body is screaming no! no, it's not fine, no it's absolutely not ok), yet you pretend and you enter the game of coping and sacrifice. As you are not truly honest you will start to sacrifice and deal with stuff you don't like and in return you will expect others to do the same just because you did. Resentment, expectations and conflict arise and if you don't get what you think is your right to be returned; you enter dangerous territories where you want to control other people, up to control what doesn't even lies in your power to control. Now the second way of this game (I.e. referring to a game to make the examples easier to grasp) is the person playing cards on table, the showdown player. This way of cards on table is the one that is honest to themselves and to the others from the get go. From the beginning there is no give and take, no sacrifice, there is only pure honesty. A straightforward way of being, saying directly what is a yes or a no, what is acceptable or not. You can hardly come in conflict with a person that is like this, you know who and what they are from day one, you know what you are dealing with. There is no game of pretend. Now you can imagine how terribly incompatible these two styles of relationships are if put together; the poker face and the showdown Player. Never this can work without suffering and pain because it's just not the same dynamic. Now maybe two poker faces can work together, and two showdown player people can work. All boils down to the recognition of where you stand. What do you communicate and how is the other person? What type are you? And what type are they? When you know how you behave in relationships, what is your style or dynamic, you can start to understand other people, other situations, like you are again here leveling up and watching all from a higher perspective. The perspective of your highest self. But awareness and recognition of the standpoints is not enough to have a healthy and strong relationship. The next step of understanding you and the others you mirror in your life is the acknowledgment of the Absolute Truth (I.e. Satya in Sanskrit). The way of being in this space of Satya, is you want to know the absolute truth, knowing that your truth you know is not true. The only way of finding what is really true is the constant study of yourself (I.e. Svadhyaya in Sanskrit) and of others. It is the questioning beyond what you believe to know or what you think you know. This can only be reached by complete honesty and open communication. There is no other way around for your evolution and inner growth. And this is scary, it is because you never know what you might find behind these questions you ask, behind this seeking and wanting to honestly communicate and understand beyond what you think you know. What you don't know can't hurt you right? Ignorance is bliss? What you don't talk about, means it's unknown, means it's for the moment still safe, means for now you are ok, you are in love and you rather not ask, so you can't risk of breaking what you have. When we find ourselves in this sweet spot of unknowing, we rather stay here because what we get in return again is Love and Connection yet again the important pillars making it ok for you to continue to suffer and stay ignorant. It's always hard to step out of the comfort zone as already mentioned in previous chapters, but this is exactly what is keeping you stuck, frustrated, angry, unfulfilled, not balanced nor in harmony and above it all, you become hateful, resentful, and judgmental on what you cannot change because of your own fears of stepping into Satya and Swadhyaya. The only right way of getting out of this downward spiral and low frequency vibrations is honesty at the highest form to yourself and clear honest communication with the others in your life. There is no possible way around if you want to get away from coping mechanisms and sacrifice. Getting rid of your fears; like you might hear it so often everywhere, is not the solution. But rather taking your fears in your arms. Just like you would hold a tiny little baby in your arms, when you are holding your fears in your arms, rather than suppressing it and trying to get rid of it; you start to walk forward, step by step with you fears in your arms. This takes Willpower, Strength, Bravery and Courage in its highest forms, this requires you to go deep into your solar plexus (I.e. naval chakra, will be seen in detail in the yoga chapter) and search within for the highest form of your masculine energy regardless of your gender.

Now that you are aware of the meanings in co-dependent and independent relationship, you are aware of the dynamics of the relationship style (I.e. showdown player (cards on table) or poker face), you are aware of what it means to search for the Absolute Truth, Honesty and Communication; we will now dive into the last part which is your Boundaries. Boundaries are important if not the most important part. Your boundaries are closely connected to your thoughts and emotions, which is part of your internal guidance system. When I talk about a boundary I don't mean building a wall that is protecting you; not at all but in the contrary. It's not about shutting out, but more of letting in. And this is what most people do, they rather shut out and suppress instead of letting in, listening within and being open to the message you are receiving. What is a boundary, do you know yours? Let's say that you get angry because something was hidden from you, something was done behind your back. This deep anger, you feel is actually an information. Now because of your ego and what you have been "programmed to", this information goes in two ways. One way is the powerful anger at first, the second information will be doubt. Now when doubt kicks in, you start searching the mistakes within yourself, you think it's your fault, maybe you were not open enough, not attentive enough, it's your fault that all is happening. So, you go into medications to suppress that initial anger, because of your fear, doubt and insecurity you search for ways to take the blame on you. You then become weak, resentful and search for answers to understand why are you this way, why did this happen to you. Can't you be trusted? Is it why things are being kept from you? This will only spiral you down into lower frequencies. Actually, all is happening for you. While you are searching for answers the initial information of anger is actually your key. Yet because of our society we think it's not ok, we think we need to be strong and not show weakness. Anger is in this case the information about your boundary, meaning that one of your boundaries might be trust. In this case trust has been violated. This is just one aspect of a boundary you can have. And there are many many many others aspects... Now when you powerfully own what is in your boundary, what is non-negotiable within your core heart, within your principles you can never again doubt yourself again. You step into the space of awareness of what is your most important values in life. The act of looking closely at all your emotions and thoughts will make you into a powerful person that knows what they want in life and what they are fighting for. Becoming a doormat is no longer an option, taking the blame and suppressing is no longer an option. Your boundaries are your most important information messenger; that will always powerfully guide you towards what you absolutely want and desire in life, and what is an absolute No. Being in complete alignment with this is how you navigate your life holding a powerful compass, your powerful compass that will help you navigate the worst storms but also navigate the sweetest calm waves on the ocean of life. We as humans need to start to step into this space of allowing and receiving any messages that life will throw at us. We need to start to step into the belief that life is always happening for us, that all is pushing us towards expansion and growth. Having boundaries, owning them and knowing them, means you are powerfully taking ownership of your life and that nothing and no one can longer manipulate you towards an unwanted aspect, an unwanted Truth. This is your way of knowing why you came here and where are you going. Relationships in either family, business, friendships up to romantic ones are going to be your blueprint to discover your boundary. Life in and of itself is your teacher, the connections you create, all of what you attract is only the expression and mirror, to push you towards what you truly want to experience. If you are unaware of your boundaries, life will push in any possible wonderful beautiful way up to the worst possible hurtful way in order for you to discover it. If one of your boundaries is love, trust, connection, infinite support, compassion and understanding and you don't know this yet, you will attract people in your life that will reject you, cheat on you, avoid you, not support you, egoism and non-understanding people, So That you can awake to the opposite of what you were always wanting in the first place. Again, we enter one of the most basic fundamental laws of our universe which are the laws of mirroring or so-called laws of attraction.

What is at the end Love in a relationship? Values, visions, life purpose, the meaning of life this all is summed up in one person. These life existential questions that make you who you are, why you are here and where are you going. The spiritual work that you do step by step on your journey is your flashlight you shine in the dark woods, your journey that is tough and rough but also wonderful and magical when the skies and insecurities clear up. Life then will throw you curve balls, to always re-direct you into the chosen path of yours. But this is your path. Your way. The moment you come into a relationship, that is the moment it gets hard. Sure, in the beginning it's a honeymoon; it's all chemicals flowing through your heart, stopping the thinking mind. You go into the river of the full conscious experience, what humans all long for to find love, be loved, have connection and be included as the most important person in one's life. But what happens when the existential questions arise? After years of years of relationship or marriage, one starts to question the very meaning of life, survival and purpose that in the end pushes you towards a spiritual journey. As these questions arise, you now search for the meaning of your life and of course you want this meaning to be holding both of your lives together. While you question this, you are evolving on the higher planes and scales of vibrations and frequency. The material world seems no longer to help you answer your questions and so you need to rise higher in vibrations. But is your partner rising up with you? Or are they left behind? As you know by now from the previous chapter un- matching vibrational states cannot stay together. Does this now mean you need to be alone? Are you the crazy one? For questioning the nature of the Universe? At the risk of being left aside and alone? Is this the so-called midlife crisis? First and foremost, I believe that the so-called midlife crisis is a myth, it is called this way because people don't understand what is happening. I like to see it more as an awakening rather than a crisis. Society forces you as a young teen, to know what your life purpose is, so you follow a road you did not really from your heart intended to follow. And I'm not even going into what family or culture told you. For that we will dive deeper in the chapter of the subconscious mind. But seriously it's completely normal that in the late twenties you start to truly question your life, or even thirties or forties...

there is no age for that moment that you stop what you are doing, take a break and ask yourself what am I doing and where am I going here? Life is so short and many situations in life can push towards these existential questions. Pandemics, inflations, wars, destructions, unfairness, globalization's and separations to name a few... are life's way of throwing the curve ball back to humanity to remind you that. So back into relationships what does this mean? You are definitely not crazy nor in a crisis, but you evolve, your dreams, life directions, wishes and desire change, you change, you evolve that is just the way of life like your cells renewing, changing and dying enabling you to survive. The question here is; is your partner going in the same direction as you. Because they also change, they also evolve or either they stay stagnant because of fear, scared of that unknown or they are simply not ready yet. Look at this example like a road, it goes up, goes down (I.e. the highs and lows in a relationship). Roads can separate, go in different ways and directions but it can also stay together like a long highway going straight. Love can also be seen like a river, multiple streams of rivers, separating, colliding, streams that run parallel or run into each other and stay merged together. At the end all these water streams will end all together in the hugeness of the ocean. Just like all your veins in your body seem to be all separate but, in the end, all work collectively to travel all back into the heart. The saying of when there is love there is a way is also not exactly always true. It can only be true when the love exists equally in both ways. If one goes at war in the relationship; you cannot say that your love will save it all. It only takes one person to rupture the connection; but it does take two people to maintain that connection. There is an important question to ask here: is there love in both sides? If the answer to that is yes, then there is a way. The second important thing is communication. Both needs to communicate their values, their most important desires, wishes, dreams. We need to find a way to communicate in a way of understanding and compassion. Bulldozing with your views and opinions cannot help deflate a bursting volcano situation if one person is in resistance. That resistance needs to be dealt with first and foremost. That is the moment you let all of your positions down, and you truly go into that person's heart. This is the very core meaning of intimacy (I.e. into-me-see), you are stepping in that person's shoes, you want to understand them, see them, feel them, hear them, with compassion and highest form of wisdom and understanding. This requires to activate the highest feminine energy in you (being a man or a woman biologically). Only when you have complete acknowledgment of how they truly feel, want and desire in life you can see, feel and understand if both of your states are compatible or no longer compatible. And that's a harsh reality to admit if you don't want to be in a relationship where there always will be one winner and one loser. Where compromise and sacrifices need to be done, which only can last temporarily until one is so tiredly sucked up of all energies that the only way is the way out of the relationship. But when love is strong on both sides you always can find the middle way of United Consciousness. This is a merged Vision and Truth; just like the heart organ, or the ocean where all meets in union. This state of merged united consciousness is the key component, the holding common ground. It will hold both of your views, it will hold both values, dreams, wishes desire as equally important for the one as for the other. It's like the merging of two cells where an intersection is found. Where a merged way finds an equal win win for both parties. Instead of the I win and you lose. This is the beauty of being a human, of being able to experience all of these sad, mixed-up confusing emotions but also most joyful and beautiful wonderful emotions. You are just entering the space of getting closer to your purpose, knowing this, you can use the tools of spirituality, your intuition, your psychic powers to step into what you choose to experience with your free will.

#

Chapter Six
Rituals

#

In this chapter we will talk about some examples of rituals you can start to do for yourself, but also rituals you can create for yourself. As an energetic, multidimensional being, you need to know how to re-center yourself, recharge, and re-ground yourself. We are so much exposed to polarities, the good and the bad, the wanted and unwanted, the environment, pollution, work, unhealthy foods, toxins, chemicals, stress from other people, and the challenge of simply being human. All of these examples can take a toll on your well-being, your balance, and your mental health. This all can clutter your inner space, and as seen in the previous chapter, you want to know your boundaries, and this also includes the knowing and feeling of when it is time to calm down, to take a break in order to step into a space where your mind gets reorganized and clears itself again; where you can revitalize and where all energies can freely flow again instead of being stuck energetically and physically. That's the reason why mindfulness is so important; it's because people get so caught up in the daily routine and forget when it actually is time to slow down. When you are fully stressed and tired, what do you do?

You sit on the couch and maybe watch some TV. While you might think that it's relaxing, depending on what you are watching, you're just feeding more information and more input into your brain and thinking mind. What about those who want to read a book? Again, here, depending on what you are reading, you might again be feeding more information instead of winding down. Some people also like to go running or exercise, now this is also a very good thing to cleanse all the toxins out and live a healthy lifestyle. But as your heart is pumping again, your system runs in a sympathetic mode, feeding all muscles. Still, your mind hasn't calmed down because maybe you have some music playing or distracting thoughts...If you don't have a ritual that really brings your body into parasympathetic mode (I.e., we will see this in the yoga chapter in depth about what sympathetic and parasympathetic modes are within our autonomic nervous system in the body), you are constantly running the body in full power mode and not giving it a break. When people say well, I get a break when I go to sleep; I like that one...how many hours do you sleep then? If again there you get deprived of full sleep, you can start to play dangerous games with your body. Also, be aware that our sleep it's the moment that healing, growth, and repair occur within your cells. Depending if you had a late heavy dinner, the night is short and restless, then sleep might not be the best choice as a recharging ritual. Our bodies are wonderfully intelligent, and they always will tell you when something is going wrong. You will start to have more and more headaches, back pain, neck pain, digestive issues, eczema on the skin, and so on... these are all indicators asking you to take a break, to go inward, or saying something is not right. The more you stretch your capacity beyond what your body is actually asking you, the more you lose yourself. You lose touch with your inner reality. The only moment to take you back is the body pulling the hand break. Mostly, that will be too late because the hand break action will force you to stay in bed. Either with a disease or a serious nervous breakdown where you can no longer ignore yourself and really are forced to step down.

Now when I talk about a practice of rituals, this is again something you do to worship and love yourself, small practices to show and celebrate the love for yourself, the bravery for standing up for yourself. So, in this case, we are not talking about rituals related to some religions that also exist, but not the case here. The first ritual you can always do, which is always easy to start, even early in the morning or when you come home from work, is burning some incense. You can buy palo santo incense or use the palo santo wood sticks. This is known to cleanse the physical body, mind, and soul. Palo santo has been used many long traditions ago said to be dated by Inca times. It was used as a powerful medicine treating ailments related to the physical body but also the energetic body, releasing blockages, tensions, and negative vibrations. The old tale says that the wood could only be taken as the tree has fallen down on its own, which makes this even more precious and related to nature, as it is retrieved from the ground and not by cutting the tree down. Now, while you let this smoke cleanse you and bring your frequencies back to their harmonized level, you can watch the smoke visually doing a dance in front of you. As you concentrate just watching how the smoke moves, spins, and twists into the disappearance of your visual field, the more you just sit there and watch, the more it feels as if you are being hypnotized. Your mind enters a transcendental state, a space of pure awareness of the present moment you are observing. While this all was happening, you noticed for that entire time that you had not had a thought. That's when the benefits of this little ritual of its own start to make its magic over you. The thinking mind and identifications subside, and you become one and unify instead of the many voices in your head. When this space of inner peace is attained, you start to connect with your inner essence, a connection to the infinite source of information that surrounds us constantly. To name a few examples of what is happening, this connects you then to the activation of your creativity, healing and promoting cell growth and regeneration, complete inner calmness, relief of anxiety and fears, and finally, negativity and anger dissipates. While you are fully present in your ritual, this is also the best moment to do some inner work, such as journaling or contemplation up to any creative work. Because you are in such calmness and peace, inspiration, intuition, wisdom, and insight directly come to you effortlessly as if you were in a powerful process of an unexplainable download. You can also use this ritual of burning incense by surrounding yourself with crystals and stones

(I.e., effects and understanding in detail will be seen in the coming chapters) and by sitting on your couch comfortably. Mostly, when we go sit on the couch, the first thing we think to do is take out the phone, scroll on social media, or pick the remote to watch TV and, even worst, watch the news. As already explained, this is only feeding more information, and you cannot effectively really calm your busy day and wind down. It's so easy, and no one really thinks about it, but the simplicity of just sitting down with a cozy blanket and just doing nothing, observing your visual space around you, is the highest benefit you can get instantly, rather than leaving the house and going to a spa or massage. We also hear that shutting all of the senses is beneficial, which it is; in the yoga chapter, we will dive into that in depth. But in some cases, activating all of your senses is highly beneficial for you.

The best what you can use here, where all of your senses get activated and used in a calming way, is the ritual of drinking tea. In this case, making yourself a little tea ceremony can perfectly be done just by yourself, with a friend, or in a group setting. Tea ceremony in the Japanese tradition dates back to the 9th century, taken from a Buddhist monk from china. They even have since then a special little tea sanctuary in the house or backyard specially used just for the occasion. Inviting someone to take part in the ritual was, in this case, an honor for the invitee as the tea ritual for them up to this day was more than just a hot drink, but rather represented purity, tranquility, respect, and harmony and a very deep dedication of presence during its preparation. Which kind of tea you want to use in this case is purely your choice; there is a large variety from calming to stress relief plants used in tea; the importance here is more of being fully present. Presence in the way you hold the cup and feel its warmth, the smell of the fragrance, how you watch the evaporation up to the taste of the flavors. You are so immensely immersed in your little ritual of your own that the rest of your thoughts or stress just do not have space any longer within your consciousness. If you are not a tea person, or you might not feel attracted to this type of ritual, what about stargazing? This is usually something again we don't usually think about doing. In the skies at night lies the biggest mysteries of the universe. When you start to look at the star's constellations, your attention gets sucked into this immensity. Any possible problem you might have suddenly feels so small and insignificant compared to the infinity of the universe that stretches above you. We are merely a speck of dust in all the united beaches of the earth, in comparison to Earth's size in the universe. Not only can we be mesmerized and hypnotized by its large scale we become the tranquility itself while watching the huge silent darkness. Also, many, many questions arise, such as the mystery and worship behind the stars. Many thousands of years ago, ancient civilizations in Peru, Mexico, and Egypt all built their pyramids and structures in alignment with these constellations. For example, the constellation of the "Orion belt" and its three diagonal stars align with mathematical precision to the supposedly three pyramids in Giza. Though still debated today and yet to be fully understood by astrologists and mathematicians. And so, we can just watch this huge mystery, feel tiny small and observe in silence, and feel how we merge to become this vastness and silence ourselves. While we are talking about the universe, stars, and being outside, how close can we get to nature and create little rituals with the Earth? We could start by taking a walk at the beach, woods, in nature, simply reconnecting with the beauty of the earth itself. When we do take a walk, let's take a conscious walk all by ourselves. This can be a ritual, too, the fact of connecting with no music, no friend, no dog. Just you by yourself and the path you are walking. You start to walk, and at first, you might hear your own footsteps on the leaves or shores and you might even hear yourself think too loud. This is perfectly normal, especially if you have never had mindfulness rituals; the brain is so used to being constantly in a drive mode it has a hard time coming down again. The best way to come back and ground yourself back into nature is to stop walking. Take a break from the walk, stand still no matter where you are, listen to your heartbeat, close your eyes, and listen to the wind or birds. When a thought comes up, acknowledge it, then let it go. You can say: "Thank you thought for coming to me; you can now go back from where you came from..." Deepen your breathing and finally re-open your eyes. Try to see what you are seeing as if you were seeing it for the very first time in your life. You will, in time, find a deeper and deeper connection with your surroundings as you are in nature; you will connect so deeply that you can feel what it feels like to be a tree. To dance with the wind, to be a home for all of these different types of insects and birds. You will feel how your roots stretch undergrounds, how you are grounded and connected to resource yourself with water, bacteria, and all of the underworld magic, mirroring the upper world above the soil where you meet the air and sunlight. You connect so deeply that you become the energy; you merge in this information field. This is how you recharge and revitalize once again with this ritual, your mind-body-soul connection. In union with nature, you become the union within instead of being fragmented, and this practice, once again, is just one way of bringing you closer to your inner essence within.

It is no surprise that we humans feel so revitalized, happy peaceful after a shower, a bath, or even just being under the sun. The water we shower with carries all of the source information while it is healing and cleansing. So, water doesn't only act as a cleansing conduit physically but also mentally, emotionally, and energetically. Many insights have been found while people were under the shower due to its informational source frequency. The same goes for the sun. The sun is the highest light source power, and it immediately interacts not only with your mood but with all the serotonin production hormones. The moment sunlight hits your skin, and your eyes, so will your brain, and the pineal gland produces serotonin. These powerful hormones regulate mood, emotions, appetite, and digestion. Not only that but serotonin is also used to produce another hormone called melatonin, which is the hormone that helps promote sleep, regeneration, and reconstruction at the deepest cellular level. While the healing of all cells and organs happens as you start to wind down and go to sleep, simultaneously in sync with your rhythm, the sunlight turns into darkness to reveal a different view of the now-dark sky and stars. Again, here, we can admire our connectedness with nature with all its cycles that allow us to thrive in life. To live a healthy, balanced life. So, take this as a part of a very conscious ritual. When you sit under the sun, close your eyes and feel its warmth and energy. Breathe it in consciously, recharge consciously, and be grateful for how it revives you, energizes you, it gives you all the needed vitamins to support healing and powerful infinite immunity against any viruses or bacteria. As you take the light in, feel how it reverses any disease in you, how it burns and shrinks any tumors up to its disappearance. It is again no wonder why light therapy is scientifically proven to heal and re-balance. Yet, strangely, society tells you that the sun creates cancer. The pharmaceutical industry might just want to keep us weak and closed inside our homes. So, we can buy their products to feel good again. But it is highly beneficial and encouraged for you to reconnect with nature as it gives us all we ever need and will need up to its sacred plants, which we will see in the plant medicine chapter. Don't let anything or anyone take your powers; that's the reason why rituals are so important because you come again closer to your very own highest powers, which, of course, agencies thriving on someone's weakness would not want. This ritual with the sun can also again be done with water. When you drink water, pour it into a glass and bless it first before you drink it. There are many powerful studies to be found about this, such as mind over matter. Dr. Masaru Emoto was one of the first to perform these studies about blessing the water and intentionally modifying its structure. He added water on rice grains, and made a batch of three containers. One he gave love and attention, the other jar he gave negativity and hatred up to finally, the last jar of water with rice grain was left completely ignored. As the study went on, after a few weeks under observation, the loving jar turned out to be fermented like rice milk, which had a pleasant and sweet smell to it. The hated jar turned out to have formed molds and some kind of fungus. The last ignored jar turned even worse, the color was darkened, rotten. Upon this observation, he realized that the intention of what was transmitted was being received by the water and affecting its content. Other studies where reported that monks who blessed water and made prayers by intention and willpower successfully lessened the bacteria level, up to transforming filthy water into drinking water. So why not try this for yourself, with your love and power of intention to bless your water or whatever you are drinking or even eating. Make it a ritual as you put your intention and love in the water you are drinking; feel in awe and gratitude how it is making you healthy, peaceful, or regenerated. Be grateful for every sip of it, and feel how it all is already happening. Feel all the good intentions you have decided for yourself. Sun and water are free energies that are always available to you. Use them accordingly to create powerful healing and regenerative rituals of your own, and just let yourself be guided by your own intuition.

The rituals you decide for yourself to do are based upon your very own will to heal, re-align your energies, and re-center yourself. This can go from meditation to mindfulness practices of being fully aware in the "Now" moment to yoga, self-caring actions, journaling, or crafting (I.e., writing, music, art, painting, gardening, poetry, pottery). Some like just to take a bath, or hot tub to flush toxins out while sweating. It is just up to you to choose what you really want to do as a ritual. But one needs to realize how important rituals are. If you don't take a break to listen to what your body, mind, and soul are yearning for, how will you know when it is time to stop? Mostly, only in times of crisis, of deep pain, sickness, depression, or severe burnout are we pulled to stop and step out of the train of the busy life and seek inner help and healing. That's the final resort the body pulls for you to wake up. But does it always need to go that far? Do we really need to feel the deep pain, the terrible stress, or the disease (I.e., dis-ease) in order to say: ok, now I need to look after myself? So much are we humans pulled towards the next goals, next steps, and next thing that the reward mechanism part of the brain keeps wanting more and more, and this brings to an endless spiral of the never-ending quest for happiness. But what if your happiness and inner peace have always already been in you, inside you all along? All we need to do is just to stop doing what we are doing. To just go inward again. Closing the eyes and discovering that there is another world upon what is unseen. That deep within we can access this Truth, the essence of a vibrational, frequency flow, like a vortex of energy and moving patterns in your mind's eye. An unseen reality that gives you access to healing, regenerating powers, and astral travel to other worlds and dimensions. What we merely see when we open our eyes is only merely a tiny spectrum of what the Universe at large has to offer. Rituals you do, whatever they are, should be able to ground you and offer new possibilities to the limited thinking and bring you forward toward the infinite mind, closer to the inner essence you truly are. The longing of so many questions, the path alchemists went to find the Absolute Truth, can be accessed within yourself. Have gratitude for the now, the present moment that you are alive. While you meditate and close your eyes, hold your mala or your crystal in your hands. As you go inward, don't try to quiet the mind but just appreciate that you are alive in the here and now. With gratitude, listen to your breath, feel present and feel how your physical body moves up and down as you are breathing. Think of the synchronicities of the Universe. What did it bring you until now? What experiences had it brought you, where within the deepest challenges you have experienced retrospectively, you now can see differently? You find the gifts and growth for all that has happened for you. All your actions and reactions, all that you do, and your choices in life have brought you exactly where you need to be today. This can also be part of one of your rituals; to just walk outside, walk the world with a different mindset, a fully open and aware way of looking around you. Analyze what you see as if you were a magician, the alchemist of your life which you are. And look what messages the universe brings you. When you see a butterfly or any insect, research the spiritual meaning of it. You can then compare this to the challenges you are going through and see what hidden messages are being brought to you. When you walk around a city or a busy mall, look around. Maybe you see someone wearing a t-shirt with a printed phrase on it; what does the message say? Does it say yes, do it? Do you hear a conversation of someone on the phone talking? Saying go for it, what are you waiting for? All these little signs, as your awareness picks up upon them, take it as a response to what your mind and heart is questioning. You may find the answers around you. Remember that you are connected to the source; vibrational frequencies and energies are constantly around you. Whatever you pick up, see, whatever gets your attention is because you are an exact vibrational match for it. So, use this to your advantage. Practice the way of being fully detached from the matrix, as you look from higher perspectives around you. You have chosen this life to live, or you would not be here. And in any mundane task, in your work, relationships, or your daily days and weeks that you go through, remember to always take a break. Be like a professor working on theories and analyzing the problems and solutions. You are the exact equation to what you are wondering and teaching for. Your awareness is the key to what you are searching for in life. Don't wait to be fully stressed out and sucked on upon the challenges of life, only sickness can shake you and wake you up. Don't let it come that far. Rituals you do should be a tool that accompanies you daily. Like a log book, like a reboot of the software. Where you constantly stop, pause, and look inward at what is happening for you. The more you do this, the more you feel that you are the key component connecting you to everything, and the more you start to understand what is happening in your experience. The more you feel guided by inner forces that are unexplainable and yet to be fully understood. You start to understand the place you take in the bigger picture at large. Don't be just moved by others like in a chest game, where you are being affected by others' actions. But be the acting force. The awareness above it all, these are only the basic teachings of former alchemists and masters that have walked the earth before you. But as you use all your tools available to you, since the beginning of this book, as you use what the laws of the universe have set, you become that powerful master that is not moved or touched by the physical Reality. But you play with the realm of the unseen. You are coming closer to who you really are, and your rituals are just a small stepping stone to what you are capable of doing in this life. The more you believe and move towards your inner powers, accessing your inner essence, the more powerful your rituals will become.

#

Chapter Seven

Yoga

#

In the very first chapter, we went through the seven chakras briefly, but here I would like to guide you in depth about yoga, where I will put out the very essential practices in order to have yet another way of understanding life as humans; where we can again use powerful tools to go towards an ending of our suffering. As an entire book can be written just about Yoga, this chapter will really condense and concentrate on the most important aspects of it in a nutshell, so to speak. Yoga means Union, but it's not what you might have heard of uniting mind, body, and soul, which is already united, but more of finding Union within the All in existence. The ultimate realization of the infinite Oneness that includes all there is. And that is the practice of yoga; so, what you might see as postures (asana) is merely just one tiny aspect of the entire

120

philosophy of yoga. According to ancient Vedic scriptures that were found, the teachings were passed orally and dated back to between five thousand to ten thousand years ago. Within the physical body, in the ancient book of Vedas, the concept of god was spoken, but not as god in religion but as General Organization and Destruction (I.e., G.O.D). These are the basic principles used to keep the physical body healthy, along with Ayurveda and the process of eliminating toxins and keeping the body in a healthy circle of renewing its elements. When people had aches in the body or any traumas or blockages, they went to see a Yoga practitioner to heal their ailments, as yoga was before and still is a powerful physical medicine, spiritual practice, philosophy, path to awakening, lifestyle, and holistic well-being to follow and practice. When we talk about the postures (I.e., Asana), this means actually being able to hold a position in a comfortable and steady state of body and mind (I.e., in Sanskrit: asana means "Sthira Sukham Asanam". Nothing to be compared to the mainstream shown on social media today. 500Bc - 200Ad Patanjali, a Hindu sage, author, mystic, and philosopher, wrote the yoga sutras, the yoga school of thought, and the inward journey to consciousness: the eight limbs of yoga. These eight limbs are 1: Yama, 2:

Nyiama, 3: Asana, 4: Pranayama, 5: Pratyahara, 6: Dharna, 7: Dhyana, and finally 8: Samadhi. Yama, the first limb is all being about the improvement of your personality. There are actually twenty- seven existing Yama's in the old Vedic scripture, but the five most important ones are Ahimsa (I.e., the practice of non-violence), secondly Satya (I.e., you are always searching for the Absolute Truth, knowing that your own truth is not true), thirdly Asteya (I.e. non-stealing, taking without an exchange or taking benefit of a situation), fourthly Brahmacharya (I.e. not indulging into the senses, wanting more than is enough, being overly blinded), fifthly Aparigraha (non-collection, how much is enough, how much to you really need?). These five little ones are truly the ones picked from the scriptures that move one toward awakening if practiced seriously as they detach themselves from humanly behaviors and move more towards searching the truth of their own existence. One of the very most important teachings of yoga being: what is real and unreal? What is permanent and impermanent? What is real, one can say, has no form; it is conscious and has a soul, which would be permanent and infinite. The unreal would have a form, and form can always change. Therefore, its state would result in being impermanent and so seen to be unreal. By only reading these lines, you can see how deep the teachings go.

Let's now dive deeper and take a closer look at the second limb of yoga, which is Niyama. Just as we now know, what you practice daily becomes first a repeated ritual, then transforms into a habit, which reflects into becoming an automatic behavior shaping your personality; and this is exactly what Niyama's are about. These are the rules and habits ones follow on the yogic path. Again, here are five steps, the first one being Shauch. Shauch is all about cleaning and purifying the physical body (I.e., daily hygiene) and mind (mindfulness practices, mala prayer, positive thoughts, clean and clear mindset). It seems this might be normal, but we mostly don't think about going deeper into just taking a shower, and off the day goes. The reason why so many get stuck on repeated unwanted behaviors is exactly because of the repeated actions they automatically do. But since we are now deeper in this book I believe you have noticed by now how important it is to constantly work on the mind. Since we also notice a lot of problems, the stress we create is always mostly starting from a mental point of view. No matter if it is thinking about an unchangeable past or an imaginary future. All starts in your mind, so why not re-arrange, clean it, and analyze it in a deeper practice? Second Niyama is Santosh (I.e., close to contentment) this means you are grateful first for what you already have. You see and hear gratitude practices everywhere not knowing this has actually been based on yogic principles. Being grateful is one of the highest vibrational states one can reach; therefore also highly beneficial and effective in manifestation or healing practices. Gratitude is not just to be seen for the little steps, it's very powerful and can change anything in your perception of your reality. Let's say it's raining, and you feel annoyed about the weather; it is already having a negative effect on your mood, which in return will make it easier for you to fire up on other annoying things since you were already in a bad mood in the first place. It won't take much for you to be affected by others or any situation. Now, what about if you watch this in a state of gratitude? You see the rain as taking a shower under a cloud. Your mood is uplifting, and you are just grateful for the weather and the relaxing sound the rain drop brings as they fall on the ground or on the leaves of a tree. Now, here, one might come to you and start whining about the weather, while you can lift them up with your totally different view of reality. You now are more of the cause rather than the affected. This is just a tiny example to show how gratitude plays an important role. But Santosh is not just the act of gratitude or the state of being happy with what you have in your life right now; the principle takes it to the next level by saying yes to all that while you keep working towards what you want. This second part of you working towards what you want is what will ground you back to reality. A practice of balancing the gratitude in the now, but not only seeing all the world around you in just pink colored glasses (I.e., all filtered by just the good & positive). It's accepting the entire spectrum and taking action from where you stand. Balancing gratitude with your goals towards which direction you are going is a mastery in- and-of-itself; one can achieve this by practicing the acceptance of what is the reality in the present moment. What do your thoughts and feelings say? How you can first accept what is and integrate it in order to shift into the next state of being ready to take action. The third Niyama is Tapas (no, this is not a Spanish dish...). Tapas means restricting yourself, but not in the way of self-harm or pushing one's desires away, but more in the sense of self-discipline. This actually requires action and bravery from you to step into the uncomfortable while you go towards getting rid of bad habits and old, undesired patterns. Mostly we just complain and keep thinking that we are stuck. This is actually you not being honest with yourself. But we stay in that place of uncomfortable "comfort" because it is the space of the known. When you know what you are dealing with, you know the usual pain; it's not something new to you, so it is easy to get lost or stuck in that pattern. But change can only happen when you leave that secure, comfortable space. In order to do that, you need to step into real change, which requires changing the old you, the old same repetitive conversations you do with yourself in your mind. And so, this restriction is pointed towards those old, perfect, repetitive excuses you create and make you move towards your desired vision; so, you start step by step creating new habits, new patterns that will shift your reality into what you rightly deserve. Moving on to the fourth Niyama named Ishowar Pranidhan, meaning you are always connected to your highest self or God (we will dive deeper in detail about that in the final chapter), but mainly Pranidhan means connection. What is meant here is that you seek to come closer to that connection; you want to go towards being aligned or in alignment with your highest self. The reason you do mala, rituals, contemplation, and journaling is pointing toward that. We are innerly seeking peace or trying to understand who we are; we want to heal, change, experience, and expand and this is a process done step by step. But the key here is first to seek alignment that will be the starting point of your journey. Lastly, the fifth Niyama is Swadhyaya, broken into two words: Swa, meaning self, and Dhyaya, meaning study. So Swadhyaya means the study of the self. This self-study is the pursue of the larger questions in life, but also seeking into who are you in the larger picture of the Universe. Just as Socrates, the Greek philosopher, coined "know thyself," I believe that he was pointing towards the quest of what we humans are here for. What is it about our thoughts, emotions, and feelings? Trying to understand ourselves better, why we suffer, up to why do we do, what we do. The seeking to know yourself is also the strapping off the many layers of our psyche, social programming, and environment. These strapping-off layers are similar to an onion, layers by layers to just find the inner core of your existence. I believe this fundamental question is the very thing bringing you closer to consciousness and awakening, and this then goes yet again hand in hand with the fourth Niyama Ishowar Pranidhan, where you seek connection and alignment, this only to go back inwards into knowing who you are.

We will dive deeper into that in detail, but you may realize now how all is making sense and how slowly all builds up. We now have discovered what the first limb of yoga is, which is Yama (and it's five subtypes), and as well as for the second limb of yoga, which is Niyama (and it's five subtypes), it is said that when one practices both Yama and Niyama are practices daily, this is the fastest way to balance out all of your chakras.

This brings us now to our third limb of yoga which is Asana, the physical aspect you may find in social media or classes. This is what people always think about what yoga is. Just the physical part, as you are discovering by now, is just one little part of the 8 steps in total of the entire philosophy and lifestyle. So why do we do this physical part? As explained at the beginning of this chapter, Asana is more than just a physical posture. But as you are fully present in the posture you not only have the possibility to go inward, but each posture activates certain meridians in your physical body, and so you can work on each chakra as well. The act of the practice of yoga asana is also a tool not only for finding alignment, peace, well-being and healing energetically but also physically. Our body system is made out of two main autonomic nervous systems within our endocrine system that is the parasympathetic mode

(I.e., digestion, relaxation, sleep, regeneration and repair of cells and organs, etc..) and our sympathetic mode (I.e., heat, run, muscle activity but also stress, anger, anxiety, is summed in the fight, flight or hide mode). These systems get equally activated when practiced in a yoga flow, slow or fast pace; each specific posture will trigger the organs. The mechanisms of how this function has been seen by science in ways such as sensory triggers to the brain, the squeeze-and-release effect, and fascial stimulation, leading the blood supply back into each organ in order to replenish, nourish, repair, and heal all cells. Moving on to the fourth limb of yoga, which is Pranayama.

Pran means life force, and Ayama means expansion; so, Pranayama is the expansion of life- force, also called "Chi" in traditional Chinese medicine. Each breath taken consciously and slower than usual can transform energy in motion (I.e., E-motions) in you, as a flowing of a river letting it pass through you; this way, you are not stagnant but rather move in the flow of life. As seen in the chapter on frequencies, Stagnant water and stuckness are always, in the end, going to lead to toxic water, bacteria, and viruses; for your body, this will mean disease (dis-ease) in time. How do we let this flow? How do we practice this Pranayama?

Well, with breathing exercises, as Prana also means oxygen, which is everywhere surrounding us. Knowing how to breathe and hold the breath (I.e., contracting 3 locks of "bandha") calmly inside will then purify your energies in your body. The locks being at the root, solar and throat chakra (I.e., our bodily sphincters such as the anus, stomach, and throat). An ancient traditional yogi quote says your life is not measured by how many heart beats you have, but rather by how many breaths you have taken up to its very last final one. To understand this, just analyze how a dog breathes and how a turtle does; one is shallow and quick the other can hold its breath under water between four to seven hours. One lives 15 years maximum or 18 depending on the dog breed, the turtle can go up between four hundred to five hundred years. Coincidence? I leave that up to you...

The fifth limb of yoga is Pratyahara, in two words: Praty, meaning anti, and Ahara, meaning food. The act of Anti-food does not mean being against food or not eating but more of not indulging and giving into our five senses in such a manner that you over-eat or are blinded by your impulses; you are in control and mastery of your senses rather than them controlling you. The practice of Pratyahara aims to not feed the five senses. How can one shut the senses down? You can practice a meditative form called Shanmukhi Mudra; with both hands on your face, you close all of your portals. The two pinky fingers go under the lips, and the two ring fingers above the lips in order to close the lips. Next are the two middle fingers that will close the nostrils slightly, just enough to let some air pass. Both thumbs will closer the ears, and finally, your two pointing fingers will close your eyelids. Deep breath in, and then you make a high pinch sound (sounds a little like a humming bee) while all portals are being closed by all your ten fingers. This practice is also called bumble bee practice due to the sound. Another way of doing this is going into a float tank. In the float tank, you will be able to float effortlessly (due to Epsom salt, peroxide solution in the water, and added UV filtration) in a closed Pod. Immersed in this silence and darkness, all of your senses start to fade away. Your body, as it relaxes, releases powerful healing, growth, repair, and regenerating properties such as oxytocin. It is said that staying in a float tank for one hour is equivalent to six hours of sleep; therefore also used for people who have trouble with insomnia or sleeping disorders. These practices are good to start getting in touch with controlling your senses, but in time, with advanced practices of awareness, you can do this in the world in your daily activities without giving in blindly to the senses. Rather, you are the one taking action over your decisions instead of falling into an unconscious state of slavery and abuse of yourself towards your own self...

The sixth limb of yoga is Dharna, which means concentration. This is often confused with meditation, which is a different practice. With Dharna, you actually learn how to concentrate. The practice of Dharna starts by choosing one single thing to focus on. Some might use the moon or a candle. Your focus is going towards what object or what you have chosen to concentrate on. This can also be done by your breath. As you sit in a comfortable position, you focus on your breathing. If this gets hard, you can use a mantra (I.e., this is a sacred word or group of words in Sanskrit, having magical spiritual powers, such as OM -activates the energy of creation/expression of the divine, or TAT TVAM ASI - oneness with the Universe, etc...) and repeat it innerly in your head as you are fully concentrated on just that mantra. Whatever your choice, either your breath and an object or a mantra, the purpose of Dharna is really just learning how to concentrate. We as humans never do this because of our busy mind, our bundle of connecting thoughts, and how it is all wired. We are constantly on the run, on the move, and so are our brains, too. Therefore, before you start to learn how to meditate, which we will talk about soon, it is a good foundational start to get to know your own mind by the practice of Dharna, by the practice of concentration.

Coming closer to the end of our eight limbs of yoga, we now will explore the seventh limb, that is, Dhyana, meaning meditation, as previously said, not to be confused with sitting in a state of concentration. As you go in meditation, you go fully inward; with maintained focus, you are being aware of the self. This state of turning inward in meditation is opening a door, a portal to another dimension of your perceived physical, three-dimensional reality. You are accessing the non-physical dimension, giving you direct access to wisdom, insight, healing, communication to spirit guides, extra-dimensional beings, and astral travel up to access the infinite source field of consciousness and information. In this mediation state of turning inward, one becomes detached from the physical body. As you find the self inside the body, the sensing of an inner presence, this presence can only be felt when breath and senses become fully disconnected. In meditation, you are realizing that inner self, when the mind is still, the body is still, and the focus is maintained, you can access and see the self. A thoughtless state is a result of meditation. This takes patience with yourself, time, and practice. Therefore, Dharna is a good way to start building slowly on your concentration, quieting the mind, letting thoughts pass and go, and listening to the breathing coming and going.

The final last eight limb of yoga is Samadhi. The state of awakening, of being enlightened. Some might call this the state of infinite Agape love or God's realization, Oneness. There exist many stages of awakening, like layers of different stages and levels one rises. We can say that Jesus, the Buddha, Mohammed, Ghandi, and many more where enlightened beings, but so are you; on your own level, reading this book as you have decided to take the path, the journey of the dark soul. When one realizes all is connected, sees with compassion, all is one, but also is aware that we live in this dimension that includes contrast, that hate and love are merely the same and that they differ only by a matter of degree, that different laws function on different planes and levels and the mastery of them, becomes such as surfing on the waves rather than being crushed by them. It all boils down to whether; are you the cause or the affected one. Or do you have that ability to rise and see any given situation out of different perspectives? To have the answer to who you are, as you seek, you simply just become. This last limb of yoga sums up the entire practice of yoga, including meditation and questioning to let you, in time, see the world without any distortion, as an important yogic principle, questions what is real and un real, permanent or impermanent up to what is the Absolute Truth. We shall dive deeper into this in the final chapter of this book.

Of course, also part of yoga we will now dive into the chakras and the masculine and feminine energies. In the very first chapter, we already have seen about the seven chakras, their elements, and qualities, but now we will see their deeper functions in relation to our organs and glands and how the physical practice is related to affect them. In order for your physical body and your mental well-being to be balanced and to function properly it is all related to our energy centers. All are located along the spine, sphere-shaped, and as thick as the tip of your pinky finger. The first chakra, Muladhara chakra, operates on the adrenal glands on the top of both kidneys. They produce hormones that help regulate your metabolism, immune system, blood pressure, response to stress, and other essential functions. The organs affected are the large intestine and prostate. When you do grounding postures such as tree pose (I.e. Vrkshasana) or mountain pose (Tadasana), the more you ground yourself back to the earth and re-balance your survival instincts. This chakra being out of balance might make you feel unstable, ungrounded, lack ambition, lack purpose, fearful, insecure, and frustrated. The second chakra, Svadishtana Chakra, operates on your gonads (Ovaries / Testes -female and male reproductive system). The affected organs are the urinary tract, kidneys filtering, and assimilation processes in your blood. Balancing postures such as the Crow pose (Kakasana) or triangle pose (Trikonasana) brings it back to alignment. This chakra being out of balance, you might feel un-worthy, emotionally explosive and irritable, lack of creativity and energy, manipulative and obsessed with sexual thoughts. The third chakra, Manipura chakra, operates on your pancreas (enzyme production for digestion and hormone secretion for blood sugar control). The affected organs are the stomach, gallbladder, spleen, liver, and small intestine. Postures to work on the third chakra will be bending postures such as classical forward bend (Pashimotanasana), classical cobra (Bhujangasana), and bow pose (Dhanurasana). An imbalance of Manipur chakra can manifest itself physically in digestive problems, liver problems, diabetes, emotional struggle with depression, lack of self-esteem, anger, and perfectionism. The fourth chakra, Anahata, works your Thymus glands, producing B cells and T cells supporting immunity by producing antibodies and invaders detection. The affected organs are the Lungs and heart. Posture related to trigger and work on this is a half bridge (Ardha Setubandhasana) and fish pose (Matsyasana). This chakra out of balance brings aggression, lack of trust, jealousy, anxiety, fear, moodiness, and attachment. The fifth chakra is Vishuddha and works on the thyroid and parathyroid glands (a hormone that regulates the body's metabolism, releasing calcium into the bloodstream for growth & repair). Related organs are the tongue, larynx, and lymph nodes. Again, here filtering and assimilation process occurs, production of white blood cells that fights infection and disease. The posture that stimulates the throat chakra will be shoulder stand (Sarvangasana) and plough pose (Halasana). Imbalance manifests in timidity, quietness, feeling weak, and unable to express your true thoughts-desire-emotions. The sixth chakra, Ajna (pronounced" Agya"), operates on hypothalamus-pituitary and pineal glands. All these three glands are the master directors of your entire lymphatic and endocrine systems. It's the government, the pharmacy of all chemicals in your brain. Organs are the brain, eyes, nose, and ears. If this chakra is out of balance; you feel lost, non-assertive, afraid of success, and egoistical; you struggle to find intuition, understanding, insight, and knowledge of the self. Physically manifested by headaches, blurry vision, and eye strain. Headstand (Shirshasana) is the physical posture to work on this. Finally, the seventh chakra, Sahastrara, is the center of spirituality, enlightenment, dynamic thought, and energy. It allows for the inward flow of wisdom and brings the gift of cosmic consciousness. When out of balance, one might suffer from a constant sense of frustration, no spark of joy, and destructive feelings. Organs, glands and posture to balance are the same as the previous chakra. To close up to the gland's function is that the Hypothalamus (regulates how much hormones the pituitary gland releases to the other organs), the Pituitary gland (releases hormones to the thyroid gland, adrenal, gonad, growth control, blood pressure, metabolism, water salt concentration in kidney, homeostasis & pain relieve), Pineal gland (lets the darkness in/out (hormones for sleep state), produce & secrete melatonin which stops the excess secretion of cortisol in response to stress, heightens immune system, decrease the development of tumors, promotes DNA repair & replication.

As for our masculine and feminine energy this is all imbedded in all existing things, beings throughout the Universe, no matter the gender. Balancing the masculine in you will help you go more towards taking action, bravery, strength, willpower, and courage to move forward despite your fears, taking loving care of your fear, holding it, and walking with it one step at a time, instead of what we hear so often to get rid of fear. Yoga teachings are not about pushing something away or getting rid of it but more about integrating and uniting everything together. Masculine energy is mostly condensed in our first tree instinctual survival chakras, in the first, second, and third chakras. Balancing the feminine is more to be compassionate, listening, openness, receiving, giving, caring, intuition and wisdom. This is also found in the heart chakra, throat, and third eye. Again, these both aspects of the feminine and masculine, this moon and sun energies within are equally important and need to BOTH be balanced by all living beings in order to transcend on higher levels of consciousness.

Final thoughts and details about yoga, and some of its many other branches and different teachings/lineages, are listed here below such as Karma yoga -> doing your dharma (duty)/path of selfless service, being of service for others, in teaching, cooking, helping in your community or the one in need.

Bhakti yoga -> the path through devotion (chanting, praying, japa - mantra repetition)

Gyan Yoga -> the path of knowledge, awareness/information processing – meditation on the nature of truth, self-inquiry, and deconstruction of mind/beliefs.

Raaj Yoga -> self-realization/mastery of the self (practiced through 8 limbs yoga & hatha yoga, meditation & cleansing body-mind-soul)

The yoga practice is not just a class that you take, a program you study, or something that you occasionally do where you revolve your life around it to find a spot where you can squeeze in yoga and practice it. No. Your entire life IS the spiritual practice; Yoga is the entire spiritual practice, not the other way around. Become the practice rather than viewing it as a moment in time. It's a discipline that becomes your routine, then becomes your lifestyle, to finally, your way of living and navigating life.

#

Chapter Eight
Crystals, Stones, and Astrology

#

Crystals and Stones - something you might have seen or heard a lot about recently in spiritual circles, shops, or conversations. Some say this is just some new-agy thing or some whoo-whoo stuff, but please have an open mind on this. Since you are anyway in your healing journey or transformation journey to become a better version of yourself, it is never bad or harmful to listen and read or talk about different approaches in healing. As you have nothing to lose but just yet again knowledge to gain that you can use as your very own personal power tools. I will share here some of my favorite quotes; I would want you to go within and reflect on how you are feeling now and how you feel after reading them. "If it scares the shit out of you, it's probably worth it"; "If you keep complaining but don't take any actions to change something about it, you are not being honest to yourself"; "You always have free will, only you can start to make changes in your life no one can do that for you"; "Dreaming but not acting is only for the dreamer, changing your life by taking radical action and ownership is transforming your dream into your vision"; "Be the Action instead of the affected one"; "In your deepest fears lies your greatest strength"; "Your life is a movie, and you are its director"; and final quote by Krishnamurti: "It is no measure of health to be well adjusted to a profoundly sick society." How did reading all that make you feel? You might feel a bit more motivated, happy, proud, or stronger. Either way, you have elevated your previous state of frequencies after reading these elevating quotes. Why am I telling you all this? Because crystals and stones are exactly doing that, they elevate your current state of frequency into a higher one. Whether in healing, power, courage, or strength, to name a few. Scientific research in the years 1880 - 1882 by Pierre and Jacques Curie used crystals such as tourmaline, quartz, topaz, cane sugar, and Rochelle salt and made a quite phenomenal discovery by conducting electricity with crystals, named since then piezoelectricity and pyroelectricity. Up to this day, it is used to power batterie as an oscillator in quartz watches, but also in LCD screens, plasma screens, LED, sonar, radio, and any transmitter technology, to name a few...this is all because of its accuracy in movement and transmission. How can this relate to humans? Well, our entire body functions on electricity, neurons giving each other signals, wiring and firing up in the brain between the neurons, and, of course, the way our nervous system functions makes the body move, think, and feel. The elements in our bodies, such as sodium, potassium, calcium, and magnesium, all have a specific electrical charge. Our human heart organ, when measured by Ecg and Ekg found to produce around 1.5 watts of hydraulic power; the same goes for an Eeg test done on the brain to detect electrical activity of 20 watts. So, you can be sure that holding a particular crystal in your hand or having it nearby affects the human body, just such as it is affecting other materials. But for the crystal or stone, it goes far beyond just the frequency and charge it carries with it. Some gems need thousands of years to form under the earth's crust by pressure, heat, water, condensing minerals, and salts. Not only that, some are formed in millions of years. Growing naturally on earth, beneath the ground. Take an Enhydro agate stone; there's water trapped in its cavity. The water in that stone dates from the Eocene epoch that's roughly 56 to 33.9 million years ago! How long do we humans walk the face of the earth? The way planets and the moon affect our human body, made out of 70% water, is also affected by natural elements such as rocks and crystals, just like we are affected by the sun, the moon, and the air we breathe. Now let's talk about structure shall we, if all this was not yet enough. The molecular structure goes up to seven crystal systems: triclinic, monoclinic, orthorhombic, tetragonal, hexagonal, and cubic. These structures can be drawn on the flower of life pattern and its repeating patterns as in the Fibonacci sequence. The same goes as for our double helix-formed DNA molecule that can also be retraced on the pattern on the flower of life and a precisely repeating pattern as well. As said, the Crystals, minerals, and stones come and grow from the earth, giving us a deeper and stronger connection to them as well as a direct connection to Gaia, our mother earth. Frequency and vibration come back in a talk here, at a molecular level of the crystals or the stones, and because we are energy beings, this will, of course, interfere and interact with our biology. That's where the power of crystals and stones works for us because it directly communicates with our energy field. And our ancestor, yet again, knew this and have used this to their benefit as well.

Burial sites where found in west England at Dorstone Hill, dated to be from the Neolithic period 10,000 - 4,500 BC, where small quartz rock crystal was found and deliberately placed beside the human remains. The nearest place where the rocks could have been taken from was roughly 160km away. This means it really had meaning and purpose to burry bodies with these crystals. This site is known to be 1000 years before Stonehenge. Not to mention tombs in Egypt, where gems were found, such as Lapis lazuli, turquoise, carnelian, and emerald, among other values such as gold, around the 14th century BC. This not only tells us how precious it was before but also that it had a strong meaning to accompany us along the path of death. The Egyptians believed that these gemstones had magical powers that could not only protect from evil spirits but also bring luck and fortune to those who carried them close to them. As far as long history goes, crystals and stones were meaningful to our ancestors, and today, that is returning. As we go back into natural medicines, as we try to get closer to nature and find new ways of grounding and healing, it seems the ancient cycles return and merge into our modern times. And so, in our modern times today, we return to our ancient roots and seek connection again with crystals and stones; we seek their powers just the same way it has been done long ago before us.

Depending on how you feel, Crystals and stones can help you with your emotions to either elevate, or either to ground yourself. This actually works in a similar way to medicinal plants. Take plants such as Feverfew, Ginkgo biloba, Butterbur, Peppermint, Ginger, and White Willow. These are all-natural plant medicines used for migraines. Actually, when you have a headache, your state of vibrational frequency is quite low from pressure or heavy down-pulling thoughts, or your state is way too high from stress and overwhelming untamable thoughts. Because these plants have a balancing vibrational frequency, the fact of using them forces your system to balance itself out and match that vibration. Therefore, as the two frequencies merge into matching each other, the headache is, in this way, forced to disappear or to alleviate. This is no way different than reading some uplifting, positive quotes or someone that makes you burst into laughing tears; no matter how you were feeling, you are immediately in that higher state, and you say ohh, that felt good, that was funny! That being said, I have to remind you here that any feelings or thoughts you have, good or bad, are never to be ignored, denied, or suppressed; they are carriers of highly important information about where your own personal boundaries lie. So, never ignore them or try to immediately change them. First, go within, accept what is, and accept your reality just as it is. When you have acknowledged your information and you have processed it, then only you can allow it to flow out in-motion and release it to re-center yourself and follow that inner compass within. Now, you can take your healing tools such as crystals and stones; some will have the properties to ground yourself: healing, protection, empowerment, psychic enhancement, accessing higher states of consciousness, abundance, uplifting, love, or indecision, to name a few. An entire book could be written on just crystals but the main purpose here is really to pick up the most relevant and important ones for starters that is a tool again to help you on your healing path. Because their powers vary from healing to release of blockages, inspiration, and protection, you should be using different crystals that intuitively speak to you for your need and usage on that particular day. Being in the presence of the crystal is powerful enough, so you can have some you will place beside your computer on your desk while you study or work on your project. Depending on what you have chosen, it will be protective against electromagnetic fields from your devices, absorb negative vibes and energy, or bring motivation, courage, and manifestation closer to work for you. Some you can also just hold it in your hand and contemplate it. By moving the stone in your hand, you can play with the reflection of the light that shines upon it; some crystals or stones will show colorful rainbow colors, or some shadows will appear and disappear. At the same time, you are watching that you become fully present, fully calm and quiet. Your state has changed; the magic has operated right there on the palm of your hand. Some might want to keep it in their pocket, or even tucked in a bra, as jewelry or by the sense of touching, squeezing, or as just discussed by contemplating it. No matter how and what you decide for yourself or choose how to use your stones or crystals, don't underestimate its powers; just being in range, near you, is already use of its powers through the information being transmitted in the energy field grid that surrounds you and emitted by you (I.e., your torus field seen in chapter matter, Frequencies, Energies & matter).

First of all, what is the difference between a Crystal and a Stone? To not dive too deep into chemical, scientific jargon, and molecular structures.

Crystals are formed out of minerals that are pure in their crystalline form. They are solid substances with a geometric form that can have a 6-sided crystal point (f.ex. example, amethyst or clear quartz) depending on their molecular structure. As explained at the beginning of this chapter, the molecular structure goes up to seven crystal systems: triclinic, monoclinic, orthorhombic, tetragonal, hexagonal, and cubic. The crystal is usually also shiny, translucent, angular, and has jagged edges. While stones, also called gemstones, are denser in appearance. That is because a gemstone is formed out of several different minerals, and it's all combined into one mass that can be round, smooth, and dense (f.ex. azurite malachite stone) and sometimes even organic materials such as wood (f.ex. petrified wood stone). As said, each crystal and stone have very powerful properties of their own because of that very multifaceted dimension they have; and also from where they were extracted from on earth. For this matter, I have picked the most relevant crystals and stones for starter, knowing that these are the fundamental ones that are perfect for starting to discover the world of crystals and stones, but if you wish to deepen the knowledge, notice that this is a separate intuitive journey in and of itself...Clear Quartz, the amplifying crystal, is the master crystal you will need to rise your spiritual awareness and energy levels to the highest degrees. Because it has the power to amplify, if you pair it or use it in combination with other crystals, it will amplify their powers and properties as well. Therefore, this makes clear quartz a valuable primary crystal you will need as meditating with it will connect you to the infinite source consciousness and universal knowledge; it is also cleansing, healing, rejuvenating, and balances all your chakras but mostly is responsive to the crown chakra. Amethyst is the charger crystal; placing it beside your other gems will recharge them. This crystal is also a powerful healer, energetically and physically. It helps you activate your psychic abilities and intuition, dissolves pain, negativity, and grief, and balances your mood while activating your spiritual awareness. Amethyst responses mostly and effectively on your crown and third eye chakra. Selenite crystal has strong feminine energies; therefore, also called moon goddess power crystal, this crystal is known for high communication, emotional cleanser, and healing. It will promote peace and tranquility, clear your confusion, and let you see the bigger picture. It is also protecting your energy field from lower vibration and external influences. Selenite is strongly influenced by the moon; it will remove what you no longer need in life, clear what is holding you back, and assist with what you truly desire, as it operates on the crown chakra. Smoky quartz is your choice to go for a grounding tool; if ever you feel too elevated, way too excited in a nervous way within your emotions; as if you could not contain it all, this crystal will help you ground yourself down again. Calm yourself down, and it will leave you in an inner quiet space so that your head and your thoughts are grounded and fully clear again. Citrine quartz crystal is your go-to crystal for manifestation. Is has a yellowish aspect to it and is very powerful as it dispels anger and replaces it with optimism. Not only that, it absorbs negativity, aids in digestion, and gives you mental clarity and confidence. This crystal will boost your solar plexus and allow for your creativity to be birthed out to the world. In doing so, you will attract abundance, prosperity, and positivity. A real little sunny gem right there in your pocket. Rose quartz is the so-called crystal of love. This crystal will connect you with your heart chakra and also the throat chakra so you can speak out of love and compassion rather than anger or fear. It will help you release attachments and move towards understanding and unconditional love. You will so then, with this, attract joy, love, and abundance because it is highly packed it the highest vibrations of love and gratitude. Pain and trauma can be healed if you allow this crystal to open your heart and re-align with your highest self and highest energies in you. Moonstones are your pick if you want to re-align with the feminine energy in you.

These energies are openness, receptivity, intuition, creativity, calmness, compassion, forgiveness, nurturing, wisdom. Physically, it can help rebalance your hormones, assimilate nutrients, and support the digestive system for a healthy, renewed cycle within. Astrophyllite stone will help you with growth and moving forward. It is used as a powerful shadow healer, helps you face your darkest fears, gives guidance and support, and protects against negative EMF (I.e., electromagnetic field), pollution, radiation, negative energies, and vibrations. As it helps you reclaim your powers back, you access insight, astral travel, and lucid dreaming as well. If you want another powerful crystal for lucid dreaming and astral travel, you can also use Lodolith crystal and Labradorite stone; both also have powerful access to mystical powers and overall healing. Tiger eye stone enhances courage, strength, power, and bravery, protection, and activates the ancient inner warrior in your DNA code (also said to ward off the evil eye), clarity in your intensions, abundance for money, luck but also awareness, and wisdom. Garnet stone activates the masculine powers, supporting also bringing courage, strength, assertiveness, action, thriving, bravery, support in the growth of regeneration of cells, and healing inflammation, energizing and cleanser of toxicity in the system. Finally, Moldavite is the holy grail for spiritual work, also called the alien stone. Coming from a meteorite about fifteen million years ago, so limited and quite rare. This crystal holds not only Earth's frequencies but also the frequency of a different planet. It, therefore, holds an intense frequency, spiritual guidance, growth, connectivity to higher realms and densities, access to other worldly dimensions, the akasha library, astral travel, and access to the infinite source field consciousness, gateway to universal understanding, and access to divine powers. On the physical level, it treats the heart and lung area, asthma and respiratory illness (caused by modern chemicals/pollution), opens and brings calmness into the heart with an infinite love feeling. I could list many more crystals and stones, but as said, an entire book could be written, and many are out there... so for the matter again, in this chapter, the purpose is to have a start of what to use according to your emotions, specific inner energies and elements within you, which we will see deeper in the astrology part of this chapter. To wrap this up, chakras that are also based on colors from (listed here in order: one to seven): Root chakra (red), Sacral chakra (orange), Solar Plexus chakra (yellow), Heart chakra (green), Throat chakra (bright blue), Third eye chakra (indigo blue) and finally Crown chakra (violet and/or white) can help you choose the right crystal to work with. Whenever you want to choose a crystal or stone that will help you re-align with that particular chakra in meditation, visualization, or quantum healing, you can make your choice based on the color of the gems. For example, Amethyst being purple and clear translucid crystals will align you with spirituality. Sodalite and Lapis Lazuli will help with the Third eye but also the throat chakra for intuition, wisdom, and connection to source consciousness, and assist with honest, open, and clear communication because of their blue color in appearance. There is a little exception with Rose quartz being pink related to the heart, but any other green crystal will powerfully operate on your heart as well, such as Prehnite, Green Apatite, Amazonite, and Aventurine, to name a few...operating on the heart meaning giving you not only compassion and understanding by moving away from unhealthy behaviors and attachments but also giving you courage, strength, bravery, self-love to speak and own your honest truth in your highest form of self-love. Cleansing and recharging of your crystals can be done with sage, salt water (notice not all gems go well in water, ex Selenite, Angelite, Azurite, Fluorite, Lepidolite, and Malachite), moon light (I.e., strongest charge and cleanse on a full moon) or leave them by a window under the Sun.

#

Dipping our toes a little bit into Astrology...

There is a special reason why I decided to add a little introduction to astrology in this chapter. Astrology has been used as the eldest form of science where astronomers and alchemists were trying to understand and re-align the mechanisms of your psyche, your heart, the physical body, look into your future, understand the placement of your dragons' head and dragons' tail (I.e., north & south node). It is said that the teachings were brought by the sky people, angels, or beings that have descended to teach the knowledge of the stars and planets. In Egypt, the temple of Hathor at Dendera was built about 14 AD - 37 AD. Also called the Dendera temple, you can find the eldest depiction of the definition of the Zodiac. The so- called Dendera Zodiac is still used in astrology and astronomy today. At some point, all of us have once been in contact with astrology either by reading it in a column or by having a reading or creating a birth chart, where you might have thought, it is weirdly pretty accurate. Fascinating ancient knowledge. If you are way too emotional, or you lack the fire to take radical actions, or you are too shy and can't speak up, these can all be understood in depth by the study of astrology. Knowing what can be enhanced, balanced or calmed down using crystals and stones; using spiritual knowledge is a game changer to understand in depth why you feel the way you feel. You may know how planets, moons constellations have their place and powers affecting our natural world, oceans, animals, and us humans too. Having the crystal knowledge and adding that to astrology how to use it on yourself and your surroundings as well, is again a very powerful stepping stone you should not be ignoring. First of all, in astrology, you also have elements similar to chakras or energy centers seen in a physical being, yet somewhat different. The elements are Fire, Earth, Air, and Water. The 12 signs in astrology will all fall into each element; this is also called the Triplicities (I.e., group of tree signs falling in one element) of each of the group signs. Let's start with fire; this element is all about being energetic, active, enthusiastic, passionate, creative, extroverted, and action-driven;

signs that fall into this fire element are Aries, Leo, and Sagittarius. The next element is earth, which brings a sense of groundedness, realistic vision, practical, sensible, security, stability, and strong will; signs that fall into this earth element are Taurus, Virgo, and Capricorn. After fire and earth come now the element of Air, bringing the qualities of communication, intelligence, mentalism, and visionaries, just like air which you cannot hold down; like a feather, it goes its wanted way. Signs that fall in this air element are Gemini, Libra, and Aquarius. Last but not least comes the element of water; just like the ocean, you might see stormy waves on the surface level, but an ocean is very deep and is quite still as you go deeper below; qualities of this element are known to be emotional, intuitive, sensitive, creative, empathic, imaginative and as said a person of hidden depths. Signs that fall under the water element are Cancer, Scorpio, and Pisces. Typically, of course, one wants to know what elements go well together (maybe for business partnerships or just relationships in general). Signs of their element always go well together with its element of itself, so f.ex. fire element with other fire element signs combines well. But also, fire is fueled by air, so you can say that fire and air signs will go well together. For a personal example, I'm an air sign (I.e., Aquarius), and my best friend is a fire sign (I.e., Sagittarius). Next is earth signs. Theses go well with other earth signs, but also vibe best with water signs. Air signs, as seen in the fire example, match perfectly with air signs and fire signs. Finally, water signs will again match water signs themselves and earth signs. Now that you have a little knowledge of the signs falling under what element, you can start to have a tiny view of what could be enhanced or slowed down while working with crystals and stones. This, of course, is just really a primitive surface-level check. To truly understand yourself and your qualities, it's best to create a birth chart. This is like a snapshot of how the universe, stars and planets were aligned the moment in time you were born. You can find nowadays easily on the internet services where you can ask to receive your personal birth chart, the information required will be the date, year of birth, precise location, and time. You don't have just one element as your sun sign, but with the chart, you will find that planets will fall in alignment with other signs as well. This will create a precise picture of how dominant your elements are (I.e., how much fire, earth, air, and water you have). This will have an influence on your inner personality no matter how society, culture, or family might have shaped you.

Astrological signs also fall under certain Qualities (that you will also be able to see in your birth chart). The qualities are Cardinal, Fixed, and Mutable. Cardinal signs are Aries, Cancer, Libra, and Capricorn. Fixed signs are Taurus, Leo, Scorpio, and Aquarius. Mutable signs are Gemini, Virgo, Sagittarius, and Pisces. The best example to understand these qualities is if you take the example of a wild outdoor race. At the beginning of the race, you are taking action; you project yourself into the environment. You are at the starting point, this is the primary thriving action and the start of the race, but still, you can be open to change... that would be the Cardinal state. Now, as you are on your path, you are single-minded in your pursuit, not easily swayed; you have a strong goal in mind that is running forward, motivated in what you want to achieve on the race track. Now, you are resistant to change; this would be the Fixed state. Finally, as the race goes on, you're getting tired, you are now open to taking a shortcut or changing tracks, you become mentally explorative, you adapt to your environment your state is now changeable and flexible. This would be the Mutable state. I won't go into the planets and their effects, nor about the twelve houses. As said this was just a tiny toe dip because I believe the knowledge of astrology with crystals combined is something very powerful. Having too much of some elements or too less, or either too much of the qualities or less, you start to have an idea again why you are stuck, why can't you speak up more, and so on... Knowing this and the use of crystal for guidance and support is a step to coming closer to your very own inner power and healing. Empower yourself and others by knowing how you are affected by the universe at large and what tools you can use by your fee will in order yet again to be the very best version of yourself in alignment with your highest self.

#

Chapter Nine
Inner biology and hereditary sickness

#

Before we start this chapter, I would first want to quote a great physicist, John Archibald Wheeler (who coined the word "black hole"). He stated, *"No phenomenon is a real phenomenon until it is an observed phenomenon. That's why, in real experiments, the properties of matter, space, and time themselves depend on the observer. Your consciousness isn't just part of the equation; the equation is you."*

If you can understand what this means you truly can understand that your consciousness is the governing process affecting your physicality. This is the very beginning starting point of epigenetic. The science of epigenetics was actually quite young, about 80 years ago. It was first introduced in the 1940s by a British biologist, Hal Waddington, and by the 70's - 80's by Dr. Bruce Lipton cell biologist who continued doing mind-blowing studies on the research. I will be going into technical details first in order for you to grasp the mechanism of cells and DNA but this will be your foundation in order to understand the actual power that you have over your body. We mostly are thought to think that we come here on earth by either chance that healthy, good genetics run in our family or that we are doomed with bad genetics, and that would be your fate, that you can't escape what runs in your family. But that is actually not the case. You are absolutely not powerless by your physical body, nor by what "runs in your family," and that is, in short, what epigenetics is going to teach you. So, let's dive deeper in order to understand this properly. Long ago, before the studies, it was believed that DNA, RNA, and protein work in a one-way street. This means that the environment signal affects the regular protein, which then duplicates each cell (RNA) like a Xerox copying machine. Your chromosome is made out of 50% protein and 50% DNA. In recent stem cell experiment studies, three different culture mediums were used to affect three identical cells in different Petri dishes. One formed fat cell, one muscle cell, and the third one bone cell. This was a primary break through that made the experiment realize that by the change of its environment, you could affect three identical cells in three different ways. This was a game changer that made science understand that DNA, RNA, and protein to not run in just a one-way street but can be affected by running in a two-way street as well. Long story short, DNA cannot longer be a simple genetic determinism. Knowing this, it's not upon DNA that can take control but rather the protein. Which is what our body is almost entirely made out of, excluding water and fat. This experiment was done with a culture medium, but if you look what is the culture medium in your system? Your DNA is the blueprint, but as it is not switching on and off by itself (I.e., not self-actualized), the medium is your blood. There are actually just less than 10% of diseases that are caused by a gene mutation worldwide, and that is Hemophilia, Marfan syndrome, Huntington's disease, Cystic Fibrosis, Hereditary Hemochromatosis, and Tay-Sachs disease. So, if our medium is the blood in our system, what is the environment that can control our cells? It is your thoughts! Thoughts are converted into chemistry by the brain. Remember, your body is made out of fifty trillion cells; they do not see the outside environment. It's your eyes, your perception of your reality, your thoughts that are the veil from the outer world into your inner world. So, what you see outward gets translated into thoughts and feelings, processed then by your brain to finally release the chemicals in the bloodstream. Therefore, the saying "what you think, you become" or negative thinking and emotions that can go up to the point of making you physically sick is not that far-fetched... Speaking of thoughts, in 2005 there was a study done by the National Science Foundation about thoughts. According to that study, 12,000 to 60,000 thoughts are what we think per day! Out of those thousands of thoughts, 80% were negative, and 95% were the exact same repetitive thoughts as the previous day. And it is mind-blowing that a lot of people do not know this. That thought is a powerful tool, and it holds so much power over its polarities that range from empowering to disempowering effects on your physicality. This is something we often see in studies and research about the Placebo effect or the Nocebo effect on the human brain. In a Placebo study, 2 groups were divided where one was given a medication, and the other group received a sugar pill. Their brains were then measured with EEG CT scans and they had their blood taken. Based on comparing the data afterward in the study, they actually discovered that there was just a 20% difference between the real medication and the placebo effect. This means the people who took the sugar pill and who believed they were taking the "real medicine" were just as effective as getting the real vs fake one. In another study the Nocebo effect was used in order to test negative electromagnetism on sensitive human beings. The test subjects were told to place a piece of plastic on their forehead while they were again being subjected to measurements. They were told that the device was emitting electromagnetic waves; measurements and reports of the people showed that they felt headaches, and differences were measured on the brain scan before and after the use of the object. Again, an effect on their physicality was measured even though it was just a piece of plastic and not some real electronic device. These studies prove to us and point towards, that the belief someone holds carries actually way more power over their perceived reality. In the end, the cells of our bodies do not know what is happening in our outside environment, but through your own interpretation (I.e., your vision, thoughts, emotions), this will transfer the information in your inner universe based on how you respond to the outer universe. Just like an interaction within the micro at a macro level response.

As we now start to understand these perceptions and the communication with our inner systems; let's dive deeper into our endocrine system. We have an in-built system that helped us survive up to these modern days of society, but this system is still the same within us about two hundred thousand years ago. As we were hunter-gatherers searching for food, shelter, and survival from predators, we already had the same functioning endocrine system, which operates in two modes. The parasympathetic mode and the sympathetic mode (briefly seen in the yoga chapter). As said, our parasympathetic systems are actually active when we sleep and digest our food, a relaxed state where our nervous system is calmed down. In this state, the flow of our blood nourishes all of our organs; our heart rate is regulated. In this state of calmness, love, or inner peace, biochemistry in our brain releases hormones such as dopamine, oxytocin, vasopressin, growth, repair, and cell regeneration. All the good stuff...Now, when our endocrine system runs in a sympathetic mode, it's the system of fight, flight, or hide that gets activated. In this state, we are fully actively prepared to run for our lives! If we go back to our ancestors, you can imagine yourself standing not far from a saber-toothed tiger. You are scared, fully in fear, and the survival mode of your system kicks in. Of course, with this perception, chemicals are quickly released into your brain. You have to think really fast, and so does your inner biology. Your cells won't go into healing or repair of your organs; if you could die soon, why waste time there? Your healing system goes fully into shutdown mode, and all the blood flow will be re-directed into your heart, which will now pump faster, and also all pumped directions muscles in order for you to start running for your life...

In this state of fear, the hormones released are adrenaline, cortisol, norepinephrine, and all related stress hormones in order for you to be quickly reactive and take direct, immediate action. Let's go back to our example and make a little short story that happened thousands of years ago...Standing in front of the saber tooth tiger, a young man named Aruun was facing two options. With a sudden, quick thought, he summed all his courage and took his weapon out. He fought the tiger and thought it was the right call. As he followed that intuition, the fight began. It was his life or the tiger, after all... with a quick rollover and all his muscles active, and he won the fight. Tired and still excited from all the adrenaline, he returned back into the village with the slaughtered animal. He now provided for many weeks of secured meat and safety from cold and hunger for his tribe. Because of this action, his bravery was honored and celebrated. In the evening, all gathered around a fire, with drums, music, and celebration. They ate and danced and had a wonderful party all together. Aruun was no longer in this state of fear and survival he was hours ago; he now returned in a state of gratitude, love, and appreciation. Hormones were now again released in his system, but this time in a state of Love and no longer Fear. Hormones that are released in a state of fear make the entire immune system shut down (sympathetic nervous system activated); the downside of this state is that if it is prolonged, it leads to sickness, disease, and eventually to death. On the other hand, the hormones that are released in a state of Love act in the opposite way (parasympathetic nervous system activated); a prolonged state of feeling Love leads to vitality, and all growth hormones are activated. The entire immune system is wired for health, healing, and longevity. I wanted to tell this story to show how that state of fear was never prolonged and constant; it always went back into balance and harmony. The way our system was designed, then and now never changed. The purpose of having these two systems, was beneficial for surviving and thriving. Animals also use this same system. When they need to survive or fight for food and shelter, they also activate these states within them. But eventually, when the "storm" is over, they go back to their natural healthy state.

We modern humans today still have the same bio-mechanically system built-in as before, but that never changed. The problem with this outside perception is that our inner system does not make the difference between a saber-tooth tiger and our boss, deadlines, husband, wife, kids, you name it. The moment we are stressed, angry, dissatisfied, or depressed we are shutting down this healing process. But do we ever switch back to love, peace, and joy? Or are we in a constant in-put of information and signals that our inner environment is picking "wrongly"? So, when disease pops out as auto-immune, and no one knows how shit started, could it be traced back into that prolonged state of unhappiness or stress? When cancer kicks in, we search in the genetic history, but what if generational trauma is causing this repeatedly? Again, today, when you go to the doctor for aches and pain, treatment and medication are used to treat the symptom rather than the underlying source. Never have I experienced or seen Western medicine questioning how you feel emotionally and psychologically and how is your work or your family environment. And mostly discomfort starts with a small head ache. Because you are stressed or worried, these are the first signals the body will show and share. Maybe we just ignore that first signal, pop a pill, and go on with working and surviving. I'm not saying with a headache, we need to go on sick leave immediately, but we need to learn to calm down again. Listen inward, our inner compass, the inner voice. Are we even happy doing what we do? After headaches that are just the beginning will come viruses, colds, and bigger health issues... Until your body literally will pull the breaks and really make you physically stop (as seen in the rituals chapter). There now, you are forced to stay in bed and take time for yourself to heal again. But does this all need to go that far? We need to go back to listening within to our wants, desires, needs, and values. Take the bravery and radical action for ourselves when inside a voice is shouting enough is enough. We need to learn how to stand strong again instead of being blinded by illusionary states of survival that only serve bigger corporations. You came here on earth with a limited time. Do you really want to live, or a you just existing for this short period of time? Our thoughts and emotions, as you understand now, are such powerful tools that act as feedback information on our cells. Our beliefs, positive or negative, have great influences on shaping our health, well-being, and happiness. Thoughts, feelings, and emotions are our internal gages that help how to not only navigate but understand our system better, in order to work with our body in symbiosis. If you take a look at stress, this would be the pressure gauge. How much pressure and steam are in there? Is the arrow moving toward the red area? We know in machinery, when that happens pressure needs to be relieved. Or the mechanism will break. Our human body is a perfect bio-mechanical machine, and you can see it the same way. When pressure builds up, depressurize it again. Find your own ways, like yoga, meditation, maybe gardening, art, poetry, maybe dancing it off; find out what is your way to bring that pressure down again. Be mindful by not adding more to it with the use of social media, TV, scary movies, or any adding in-put on the already charged system. How about anger? This would be our temperature gauge. Feels like it even, no? When you feel that anger rising up, don't you feel heat in the body? Some people even become red on the face. Here, it's some cooling down that we might need. How about a shower, or get yourself an ice cream, ice bath, take a walk maybe feel the wind on your face, the fresh air on your skin. That would be a start. Don't argue. You're angry anyway whatever one might say might not come the right way nor calm you down. Maybe when you try some techniques of your own, screaming into a pillow you can start to wind down again. Take a journal and ask yourself why that trigger me so much. Where does this pain come from? Is there a way to understand it and heal it so it doesn't explode on your face again? When you lose your shit, it's always an information carrier, so you can go within and find where that shadow comes from. What about feeling love or fear? As a little side note: I like to say that the opposite of love is fear and not hate or anger. When you love, you are not afraid of being hurt; you trust your gut and go for love. But when you are afraid of being hurt, maybe you don't trust, and so you don't love in order to protect yourself. So, what would be the gages of love and fear; it would be the power gage. How is the power on the batteries, low or high? How is your power gauge? Are you empowered (feeling charged) or "impowered" (feeling used)? How can we find ways to move more into love instead of fear? This entire book breaks into chapters, mostly by the end of the book. But mainly here, you need to go back to your inner essence, which is pure love. No one can truly take your power away, nor can you give it away. We all are powerful beings, and we create our inner and outer environments. Mainly the secret is not to learn how to get rid of fear or push it away. But with tremendous courage, bravery, and radical ownership of your own Truth, to care to take that fear like a little baby that we would hold in our arms (as seen in chapter five). Instead of getting "over" the fear but rather stepping with it forward with little baby steps. No one can take your power or free will away; it only seems so because so much pressure might have been put on you that you will choose to comply or go their way. This is just seemingly true, even in the worst states of being imprisoned, you still have the power over your own thoughts. If you chose death over fighting to stay alive, it still was your choice to give up or not, to give in or not. Death was still a choice.

Knowing all these inner gages of pressure, temperature, or power, we now see the importance of these gages and signals. Let's just take a look at your car. If there is an oil problem, the oil pressure signal will appear in your car. It will show and blink as a red signal light. That calls for an immediate stop with attention and response from the driver's side. You can't just put a Band-Aid over that signal so you don't see it visually anymore. Ignorance of this would cause severe motor damage and you can for sure throw that engine away. That's the heart of the car that u just ignored. In mechanics, this would just be a part that can be switched. But going back into our bodies, you would really want to avoid, if possible, the switching of your inner parts. And, of course, before it goes that far, yet again, you had little signals, little warning signs. Medication is just that Band-Aid that treats the symptoms, so you don't "see" it or feel it anymore...The root cause was never addressed, and unfortunately, in doing so, you are just covering the initial warning attention. Your body has an infinite intelligence always working for you; it gives you the very first signals for you to take radical ownership and action in your life. Taking the wheel of the driver's seat instead of sitting in the passenger's seat is to powerfully own that power, honor our infinite nature, embrace the signals, and reverse the disease. As I mentioned at the beginning of this chapter, we can influence our biology. Genetic disease is about 10 % (hereditary gene mutation if not received at birth), and the signal (our perception) is about 90% that then acts upon the behavior (I.e., the manifested disease). And because all does not flow in just one direction, you can, by your behaviors, reverse all actions and go back to growth and healing. One might ask, what can alter that signal? Physical trauma would be one aspect. Let's say you would fall and break an arm or a leg; bones would need to be mended together in order to fuse and re-heal itself. The primary action of this physical breakage would be the initial physical stress that is put upon the body. Another aspect of the signal would be toxins. Toxins could come from many sources, such as processed foods, mold, pesticides, herbicides, to industrial chemicals that may appear in the air, water, or household products. Our bodies will filter it out by breathing out urine, feces, and sweating. Not only that, but as already mentioned, we have such an intelligent built-up system; our liver, kidney, filtering, and assimilation processes organs will expel all toxins and heavy metals out of our system, which is not in coherence with our inner biology. But when it is all way too much, and the body can't keep up anymore, what happens is the toxins in the body will start to create a chemical imbalance (digestive issues, etc..). The effects of this would be chemical stress that has been put upon our bodies. Finally, a last important signal would be our thoughts. As said in the beginning of this chapter; consciousness misinterpreting the perceived external. Because thoughts and emotions are a direct tool that affects our inner biology, they act as a culture medium, passing information through the bloodstream up to the brain, our pharmacy that will release certain hormones. This would be the emotional stress. Work deadlines, limiting beliefs, making you believe you are in a closed box where a ceiling is put upon you that you cannot break. Such that we become blinded by an external illusion and forget our powerful, infinite nature. We then forget the spiritual aspect that holds more power over the material physicality of our universe, which is, in the end, just a creation or figment of our consciousness. The balance is forgotten and the pendulum swing goes way too far on one polarity over the other. These three signals of physical trauma, toxins, and finally, thoughts can all be brought together under one single umbrella that is named Stress. Under this aspect of stress also comes fear, anxiety, depression, anger, dissatisfaction, loss, uselessness, negative thoughts, negative feelings, shame, unhappiness, unworthiness...this could go on and on. And the more prolonged all of these states are felt, the more this is creating a chemical imbalance in your brain. When stress is permanently residing in your head and has become a habit in your body, it becomes difficult to change that. This is like a habituation to the system, like an addiction to these chemicals. Stress, in the long term, will shut down the immune system and thus shut down the maintenance of the body, which now makes one open to disease.

I would now want to dive deeper into the energetic aspect of disease in our system. Sickness, pain, and disease in our body also arise from an energetic point of view where the flow of energy no longer flows but rather stays stagnant. You now know that the body is always working for you and giving you primary signals, and there is no such thing as hereditary sickness apart from what has been previously discussed. So where could this possibly arise? We need to take a further approach to the function of our organs and glands cholesterol, autoimmune diseases, Parkinson's, Dementia, ADHD, cancer, allergies, inflammation in the body, you name it. We need to dive deep into the roots and understanding of the internal intelligence and mechanism of your body. You have the power to influence and manifest all things in existence; I know this sounds triggering, but this means you have control, whether good or bad, positive or negative, sickness or health, abundance or acceptance, to stay where you are. All in existence is bound by energy, meaning that whatever occurs can be reversed by your state of consciousness, emotions, and gratitude. But we need first to accept what is going on in our current life. Accept the pain and the grief, but consciously be aware that you no longer want to stay on a repeating pattern that no longer serves you. Before you can move on, you need to accept the situation as it is. Grief is your feeling your emotions, the totality of it. Let's say you have back pain; it is constantly inflamed, and you keep on taking medications to make it go away. Which then does, but it will at some point always come back right? What is located in the area of our lower back? We have our pelvis. This is the largest, strongest bone structure supporting the entire weight of your body. Having pain in this area could indicate you have been for a long time now the pillar of foundation everyone relies on; you have taken all the weight of all the others, buried in sacrifice for all of them up to becoming a doormat. Maybe your body is indicating to release some weight, don't carry their energetic bags any longer and think about your own health. See if the pain physically releases as you take this new approach and shift your way of being. How about pain in the neck and upper back? This area holds the space of the throat chakra. Do you honestly communicate where your boundaries are? Or do you take the burden of accepting all as it is, again carrying way more on your shoulders than you can or should?

Creating this pain and tension. I'm bringing to your awareness that your body, again, here is the map; the moment you know how you can read it, your consciousness, thoughts, and emotions will be your way to navigate this smoothly into calmer waves instead of these constant stormy waves. Your body is a deep ocean you need to start to listen to. Let's look deeper into these diseases; cholesterol, again, here is the same. It gets constricted, and blood does not flow properly, which causes a blockage that can restrict supply. This leads then to heart attack or cerebral blood clots... First, we need this membrane that surrounds our cells, we need fats, and we need HDL cholesterol in order for the cells to function; not having that wall, that membrane your cells would die. Maybe this means you need to start to create your own new circle of people, change your people's environment, that constrict you, be more attuned with nature, and eat foods that support your healing, and you will see the flow of blood will no longer be constricted. You can manage this through a healthy mental lifestyle, weight loss, and becoming a new, stronger, confident you. Inflammation in your system is just the natural way of your body healing itself, but it is up to you to recognize the "where" and "why". The same goes for Parkinson's, Dementia, ADHD, and ADD people we stamp with that we put them aside; they are no longer needed, and they do not function correctly. But wait, is that true? If an elder person was never pushed away from society and would still be actively needed, do you think they would get Dementia? Go see into other cultures how the elderly are strongly needed for medicine, advice, feeding grandchildren... I believe many of that is not well understood, people sort of abandon themselves because they literally are being abandoned by society. ADD and ADHD, if you let them be how they want to be, are people who are highly creative and intelligent in their own way. It's not a disease, but we stamp them so. Why put everything and constrict it into a box? We are all different and have our own qualities. Valuing and giving the right support might fully heal them or enhance their gifts. Lastly, I want to talk about cancer. This goes in a broader spectrum as it can occur in any organ, but what one needs to do is to recognize it. What organ, what is its function? Can we relate that function to human behavior, society, and connection? Is it how we speak? What is taking your energy? How do you refill? How do you deplete, or where did you abandon yourself? I want to end this chapter by just saying we humans are powerful, magical, intelligent energy beings;

we absolutely have the power to transform anything. Just step out of the old paradigm, that old box, and test different alternatives. What else to try if all has been tried out? Take the courage to own your truths and values. Be the next miracle they will be talking about. Be the infinite skies because the only limits that can be set are old stories or the limit of what you think is possible. So, dare to go further than what is expected to be the limit and rise above the conventional as you step into the unconventional miraculous healing.

#

Chapter Ten

The subconscious mind and reprogramming

#

You are the sun they first see on the surface as people meet you, but also, you are the moon that holds the deeper aspects of your personality, the deeper layers and hidden shadows. Astrology puts this wonderfully out with the sun and moon. But you can also take the vision of an iceberg; the tip of the ice coming out on the surface is just a small vision compared to the immensity of the ice hidden below the surface. That is another representation of your conscious and subconscious mind that we will be exploring and diving into in this chapter. Let's go into the very start, the moment you were born. You are this pure, innocent little thing that perceives its surroundings by just seeing, smelling, the sense of touch, tasting, and what you hear. You are perceiving a separate world where you slowly notice a sense of separation between you and the outer world. In the womb, you also already developed these senses, but we can say less loud and filtered through your mother. We can also approach this from a more logical sense. If you take a computer that you bought that is fully new but has no built-in systems. This means there are absolutely 0 programs on a pc without an operating system. Programmers, Gamers, computer technicians, and IT lovers know this best. They buy this blank computer because they want to build and download the programs from scratch to be specifically tailored to their own needs. And so, they will download the programs gradually in order to use drawing tools, programing tools, etc... they will install and download all they need in order to be able to use the computer. So, in this example, you then have that physical body as the computer (hardware) and then the built-in downloads (software) as the programs to be used. If you take this example to a baby, it is very similar and a bit more complex, but I guess you get what I want to convey to you. You have the physical body of the baby and its program, which is his mind. That is, for now, still quite empty. And this mind needs programs too in order for you to be able as a child to function in society and be integrated and accepted in your growing culture. Some built-in systems, like the senses, are already there, and the inner body intelligence will be there too as well; such as how to process breathing, digestion, expelling waste, and body temperature regulation, as well as the heartbeat are some basic little examples of that inner intelligence. But for the rest, you will need the download of speech, language, behavior, walking, etc... And the more you evolve, the more you will need programs in order to function in society. You will be observing details from your surroundings and observations as a child. For example, you will observe how mommy talks to daddy is very different from how mommy interacts with a police officer or the mail man. This is all very tricky and complex, but thankfully, our brain was just designed for this. So, how does this magic operate? How can babies and children pick up so fast? Here is where a very intelligent part of our system comes in. How this was designed is simply genius because all the baby or toddler up to the child needs to do is simply observe! The brain waves from 0 to 2 years are mainly just in the state of delta brain waves. To be even more precise, the delta phase starts in the last trimester in the mother's womb. This delta brain wave (unconscious state) state is mostly sleeping, but here, at this very tiny age, they already pick up emotional frequencies that were transmitted in utero

(I.e., out of epigenetics seen in the previous chapter) as well as from their surroundings. All you need to do is simply observe what is happening around you. As the brain develops and the toddler grows into a small child, the delta brain wave is still present, but now, at age 2, it overlaps with a new brain wave, which is theta brain wave. This state is now where imagination comes into play. This phase will continuously go from 2 to 7 of age. This state of imagination is the very reason why children can play with anything and make it seem real. Like using a broom and seeing it as their pony or playing pretend at tea parties where they drink nothing, cooking out of an imaginary kitchen, and talking for hours and hours about how delicious it all is. But how did they get so smart up to this age? Where did they pick those manners or behaviors? Here is the most exciting point of this intelligent system of how the brain works: both delta and theta brain waves operate in a state of hypnosis. As I said in the beginning, all they need to do is to observe the surroundings, and by this state of being in "hypnosis," the program gets downloaded super easy in the brain. Your self-identity is being built in these crucial first years of your life. This is sort of a double-edged sword, one can say because whatever you are picking up is literally being soaked like a sponge. The brain actually will start tuning into alpha waves only from age 7 until 12 (after the self-identity has been created, so to speak). This is the stage of calm, conscious understanding, and logical thinking. Now, if you understand this all correctly while you are parenting your child (under the age of 7) with "your conscious logical thinking" they will not understand that! Because their brain doesn't function yet in the same waves as yours. They are more in this intuitive, dreamy, hypnotic state, and this is what I mean by the double-edged sword. I absolutely feel that every parent did their best with how they were raised as well. But today, we have a different understanding; today, we are in the Aquarian age, things are shifting, frequencies and earth energies are rising, and so are the new births of these children. They arrive here on Earth with a much higher level of frequency. So, the way parenting has been working for decades needs to shift. It is way outdated. That is the reason why, as adults today, we seek self-help and healing. Because we want to find our power back. The critical point where self-identity was created occurred as what we have picked up in our childhood, which was wrongly understood. This made the dysfunctional adults today maybe being less confident, codependent, or narcissist. All of that is really just a strategy that has been picked-up in order to feel loved, to feel accepted, to feel part of the family or community. It's a relationship pattern they have adopted...But what message is being picked when you are being sent to your room because you don't behave as you should? Not only do you feel abandoned, but you feel not understood, and your caretakers feel just overwhelmed. And this is the easy way. Sending one away, neglecting the initial feelings or emotions. Eventually, this turns into aggression, violence, and physical or mental abuse. If you recall the last chapter, we talked about how many thoughts we think per day and how many are repetitive. 95% is your operating subconscious part of the brain; it's the downloaded program. It's only 5% that is the tip of the iceberg that is your conscious part. The conscious part of dreams, wishes, and desires. So now the question that arises is how do you know that you are living the life of a program if you are not even conscious of it? If all has just been a hypnotic download? Who is that inner critic talking in your head? These many voices. Like a team of council talking to you. We are just not framed as being schizophrenic because we do these conversations in our heads rather than out loud in public. But really, all these parts of your subconscious inside you are the fragments that you needed to create as you were little in order to be safe, to feel safe. These are your inner protector parts. So mainly, the moment you start thinking, you shift into that unconscious program, and the way to recognize it is anything you are trying to achieve in life, and you need to struggle so damn hard to achieve it, is the meaning of that old, outdated program which is no longer supporting this new version of you today. Your struggles are your key. If you look at your life today, are you leading and creating the life you want? Or have you been living a life you have been programmed into? Let's dive into the conscious part of our brains. Everyone at least has been in love, truly connected to something or someone where you do not shift into the "thinking" part of your brain. In this honeymoon phase all is so wonderful! Nothing is negative or bad; even the job you hate is awesome; you are simply in this bubble of love. You could, so to speak, go for days without food because all you need is just this love. But the moment this honeymoon phase is over, you eventually go back into thinking, into the mundane: bills to pay, regular life problems, and immediately, you shift your consciousness into that unconscious part of you. Arguments will arise, and suddenly, you will hear the other person asking you: who are you? You are just like your dad, or you're just like your mom. This is exactly because as they were interacting with you in that "bubble of love" phase, all was happening with that conscious part rather than the unconscious part. And so now when you go "unconscious," it's like they don't recognize the moon side or the shadow side of you. Here is another example of understanding that. Do you remember your very first driving lessons? You were so conscious, so nervous, everything needed to be double-checked. Your seat, the mirror, your angles, your chair up to your hands positioned on the wheel. How do you drive today? I'm pretty sure one hand, texting while eating something...ok I'm a bit exaggerating the facts, but you know what I mean, right? Everything is so automatic...everything is so on autopilot. So, who is the person driving the car? As you go about thoughts in your head, conversations with someone next to you...you got it. That is the automatic program that just took over. That's the reason sometimes you get to a place, and you're like, how am I even already here? What road did I take? The same goes for the maniac driving and shouting at other drivers. Where did that aggression come from before you then turned back into the normal "you" again? It's exactly that: the moment you start thinking or being distracted, your mind goes to autopilot, and in doing so, it runs all its known perfectly downloaded programs so that "you" can keep functioning in a subconscious way. In analyzing this we can start to understand where all the craziness comes from. It is time that the trauma ends with this last generation; as times are shifting, we need to go into a new way of conscious parenting. We want children to be independent and strong, making their own choices and feeling what they really want and need. We are not their teachers, but we have to see them as being little light warriors, and we are their guides as parents. Giving them conscious choices, letting them make little mistakes, and, most importantly, acknowledging their feelings and emotions by being compassionate parents. I feel this needed to be said as the wheel needs to turn, and if we want to end suffering, it starts with the seeds we plant, the seeds we grow. We seek to nurture not only our inner and outer garden but the garden of the earth as well. To achieve this, it can only be done by a collective rise of conscious beings.

So, if we go back into the brain waves, from age 7 until 12, it's that logical thinking, as said (alpha brainwave). But from age 12 and upward, you go into Beta brainwaves. In this state of active consciousness, you can think logically about abstract propositions, hypothetical thinking, and scientific reasoning. Which can again become a dangerous part that can bring you into a box of just being in the scientific paradigm or just the box you were fitted in. But we aim to get out of this suffering, and we need to go beyond that box, break the glass ceiling, shine the inner essence in you, to be closer to your highest self. And that next state of the brain wave will then be gamma. This is the extended, super-conscious awareness state. And it's funny because we circle back here, but it's aiming to see the world again but with the child's eye. Being able to be in a state of heightened perception, insight, and intuition. Accessing downloads out of higher realms. The state monks or advanced, motivated meditation practitioners achieve a transcendental meditative state, a coherent state where you can access mystical experiences such as DMT (I.e., we will dive a bit deeper into this in the chapter on plant medicine) release out of your brain; that is the gamma state. So here we are now, left with all these brain states, programming, inner critic, self-hate talks, judgments of not being good enough, or just willing to stick with anything or anyone, coping and self-sacrificing, becoming a doormat rather than taking the risk of ending all alone. And this all is related to that conscious and subconscious part inside you, these fragmented parts, that war inside you that you fight daily. Diving into negotiation in constant hope to win that inner war. If we subjectively take this to the outer world around us. No one ever really wins a war. It's always about who wins and who loses and whoever gets the greater financial benefits and power out of it. This subconscious part inside you will never want to settle because it exists in your psyche for the very reason of your own survival. So, there are a few steps to understand and take to deconstruct this and how we can reprogram ourselves out of this spiral to find inner relief and peace, but mostly to take back the power and control of our own mind.

Firstly, you need to know the problem and the root cause in order to change and re-program. This is part of deconstruction (I.e., similar as seen in Chapter 2). You need to know what you are dealing with first. Today, you understand differently, as did your inner child. But what self-identity has been created years ago? Where do you struggle most? And now, question that very thing? Is it really true? Because if I keep believing this shit, it is just bringing me nowhere except for feeling this constant pain. Or wherever "it" decides to pop- up out of nowhere...Einstein said this wonderfully: insanity is doing the same thing over and over yet expecting a different result. This fits exactly what is happening because the moment you become aware of that part you wish to change, you talk to yourself, and it's just not working. It's not recording into your subconscious part. Here are two main reasons why: firstly, it is your protector parts, and secondly, your brainwaves. Let's start with the first part, your inner protector. Your protector parts are the result of what happened during your crucial part of growing up. Know that each of these fragments, all of your inner parts acts as a safety mechanism. Because of that, it will never leave if "it" believes you or "it" is still in danger. So here is where the deconstruction part starts: why do you feel as if you are not good enough? Or why do you feel as if you are all alone? It all starts with that inner child; you need to dive in and understand it. Because what you believed years ago is not only true as you picked it up from hypnotic brain states instead of the conscious state but also mainly that belief you hold, that inner child in you, is still there and is still in the state of being misunderstood. Bulldozing yourself is not the answer. As you start to understand and comfort it, you integrate these old wounds, and from there, healing can start. Secondly, you can be grateful for all of the shaming, the programming, the abandonment, and the judgments because all of that has just been a projection of your caretaker's own shadows, traumas, and beliefs. It was never yours to begin with. By understanding this not only can you find forgiveness and healing for yourself but also for anything and anyone that has ever hurt you. You could say that they were your universal mirror teachers. And to me that is a gift where one can start to find strength and power instead of being victimized. Integrating all these fragments is finding the source power in you as you process it all by alchemizing the magic in you. Now that you have cried, you have processed it, you are on the path of healing by integration, and you understand what program needs to be updated.

Now is the time to change, and for that comes the 2nd part, which is your brainwaves. You know by now that talking to yourself and wishing for change is not working because of how your brain works. Let's go back to age 0-7 when you picked up everything like a sponge because your brainwaves were in Delta and Theta brainwaves, and today you are operating out of Alpha and Beta, so yes, you can keep on talking and wishing, but it will not be registered and imprinted the same way. Okay, you may now say, but you kept learning since then, right and that worked! Yes! Let's go back to the example before of driving a car. What happened here is that in doing so, daily, monthly, and yearly it became an engraved program, and the reason is due to habituation and repetition. Imagine how it would be if you would need to learn again and again how to walk every day as you get up and out of bed. How does that sound? Crazy right? You learned it as a toddler, wobbly standing and trying, falling over and over again and restarting until you learned by repetition... Repetition and habituation is one way of reprograming yourself, and you can use the mala (I.e. chapter 1) to help you do so in a very mindful, conscious way. Set up for yourself daily rituals and ways to reframe and reprogram these limiting beliefs. Habituation is a strong way of re-programming; as soon as you are used to something, it's hard to re-change that, right? Another way is hypnosis, right? If that worked back then, it can work again. You don't need to go to a hypnotic therapist for this. Delta and Theta operate in your sleep; as you start to wind down, you go into that mellow state up to falling asleep right before waking up again. You can create a recording where you talk to yourself and so reprogram yourself when you are in these states of consciousness. The state of shock is another way that will kick you out of the subconscious program. What I mean by shock is some kind of realization of your limited time here on earth, a so-called existential crisis that sets you off into radical awakening. This could happen by an extreme event such as a pandemic or the diagnosis of a life-threatening disease. No one wants to experience this, but knowing you are put on a death sentence where weeks or months are counted, you won't want to waste one more minute of your life. This is a powerful game changer horrific yet liberating at the same time because what is here left to lose? And so the easier you will start to detach yourself out of your old life. This will kick out any subconscious program, including the ego because you are faced with the reality of your now very limited time. This shocking news is a straightforward bulldozer that will shift your reality and will push you to let go of any unswerving patterns in your life. You might quit any illusions you were bathed in and will go do the things you always wanted to but never could out of fear. Fears, limiting beliefs, and programming that were holding you back will all fall down like a house of cards, and you will have all the courage to move toward your last bucket list. Fun fact: most people who do make this jump end up having spontaneous remissions and miraculous recovery. The last part of re-programming will be the state of necessity, what will be inevitable. You know, by the nature of the universe, the realization of unsustainable systems will end up collapsing. You can see this in nature, our earth, to government systems. If something is not in harmony, it inevitably goes into the next phase of collapsing, bringing forward the need to go towards destruction in order for new birth and new creation to take place. Many earth cycles of civilizations and natural catastrophes have shown this. Shifts happen as they enter into new cycles and where old cycles come to an end. This process is even happening in your inner universe at the micro level when your cells need to destroy themselves and renew in order to avoid the state of being stuck which would then lead to disease. As you know by now, it is only in a state of flow and moving waters where life can thrive, and that is totally the opposite of stagnation. For that very reason, this is going to be your very own pushing point. When you realize that you cannot longer be living in this state of unhappiness, this state of as if something is missing in your life, you will be pushed inevitably into expansion. You will feel that inner stagnation and that the only thing you know and need to do is to be moving forward. That expansion will break your seemingly illusionary glass ceiling, and you will find all the power, motivation, courage, and strength to change your life no matter who, what, or where.

Now, while you will do the work to re-program yourself and change the limiting beliefs and unswerving patterns, you will encounter challenges during the process. Techniques that can be used to de-stress, calm down, re-focus, let go, and ground yourself again are listed here below:

Breathing: When you get brought out of balance get annoyed or angry. This is one way of always coming back to you, to remind your body to calm down. Breathing in for 8 seconds and breathing out for 8 seconds signals the nervous system. It's all ok, you are safe. So you can relax again from what has triggered or annoyed you.

Observing the thoughts: If you get triggered or annoyed while you are in a conversation, you can always observe the rising feeling, the rising thought, and realize that it is not you, but it is a primary reaction coming out. Of course, if the feeling is too strong you already shouted and attacked back before you could observe yourself. Remember: observe the anger so you do not become it. But also notice that angers and triggers bring information about our inner protector fragments; here is an opportunity to dive in and deconstruct what that information is and how it can be healed so it no longer needs to be re-surface. If breathing or observing is not working due to the uncontrollable emotion, Eft might help.

EFT (Emotional Freedom Techniques): When emotional energies are far too strong and become uncontrollable, this can be applied. You clearly cannot just close your eyes and try to breathe slowly when you feel like you can't breathe and an anger-aggression volcano is erupting in you. EFT helps treat severe anxiety, stress, trauma, and PTSD (post-traumatic stress disorder). According to Healthcare International, a scientific, peer-reviewed journal published in 2018, they observed remediation of clinical PTSD symptom levels in between 84% and 90% of veterans.

Guideline start: tapping with the middle finger on top of the head, then continue tapping on the eyebrow, side eye, under eye, under nose, chin, collarbone, sternum, under arm, left and right (karate chop). Repeat until you feel you are ok again might take 2/3 times tapping repetition. The brain is wired with electric signals firing and wiring; if it undergoes negative emotions, it will release chemicals. Direct touch undermines the process. Like a ctrl + alt + delete force quit. It will prioritize EFT to the strong emotions. As the brain cannot process both signals simultaneously, touch will be the priority of the brain.

It's not an easy journey on the path of spirituality, awakening, and freeing yourself from illusions and what is holding you back. By now, you must have encountered recurring behaviors or patterns that always came back up. It's not always about working hard, but it is about realizing and recognizing where you are stuck, where your ego always gets hurt or resurfaces to attack others in order to protect itself. Remember where you struggle in life, is your key and means you are operating from a subconscious level. Is the struggle about money, relationships, trust issues, fear of being alone, weight loss? Look at your childhood. Do you recognize similar patterns? How about your parents, culture, society...? See the mirrors; in challenges you meet are what is being reflected upon you, to call for recognition and change. A lot of trauma and programming can also be traced as far back as your ancestry, your lineage, and the bloodline running through your veins, encoded in your DNA. So, healing that old program goes as far as healing the ancestral shadows. In the final chapter you will understand deeper about ancestral healing. It is challenging to accept what we want to change because we are scared internally. The approach needs conscious communication with not only your own traumas but also with your responsibilities and loved ones. You might think following your inner compass is letting them down, but they grow and get to expand because you are doing that inner work of re-programming. You need to find mediation and a conscious, compassionate approach and finally step into a win-win scenario rather than sacrificing and staying stuck in your old ways. But in the end, the choice of taking that turning point will always be yours and only yours to make to get closer to your personal growth and well-being.

#

Chapter Eleven

Evolution

#

"Who are we but the stories we tell ourselves, about ourselves, and believe?" quote by Scott Turow.

Evolution is, in a sense, the expansion of how you can grow and then change into something new. That is the reason I wanted to start this chapter with that quote by Scott Turow. What is our story in this story of human evolution? We want to know these questions, which we will dive deeper into in our final chapter. But before that we need to see the perspective of our current reality, the stories we have been told. It is only when you have been given a key that you can open a door, and in this particular chapter I want to challenge your curiosity, the possibilities of what if the stories we have been told no longer hold truth in the newest paradigms. As questions are being asked and studied, we discover and unravel new approaches as more people, science, and research challenge and seek to find a response to the old story we have been told. That story was told 150 years ago, in the 19th century, by Charles Darwin; the theory of evolution is that we have evolved out of the primates through a process called "Natural Selection", meaning the inferior species will not be able to exist or survive under the stronger one. A science based on the survival of the fittest, which has been leading since then into competition and conflict. This has been our model up to today, and it forced us to be in constant competition. Which country has the strongest power, who is the "fittest", and who has more control...we have been pushed into mechanisms leading to wars, fear, and hate, separating humanity and creating these borders and lines instead of uniting and empowering humanity. But why empower humanity if we believe that old story? We are just here based on determinism, in that thinking of nothing really matters; we take everything for granted. There is no respect for the beauty of our universe. How everything is interconnected, as you are just here because you evolved by chance from a primate into a human, so there is nothing special about your existence. All that matters is more power, more materialism, and competition...so the old story...so the old thinking...

This makes one ignorant towards the wonders of the world around you and treats nature and animals with no respect because you think you have to survive. So, you take all the resources of the earth, suck all energies out, and don't think about fossil fuels, any destructive behaviors, or your imprint on the earth. Animals, resources, to even people are just here to meet your needs because you are the highest, strongest power in the evolutionary process. You do not care about others nor about how everything interacts or communicates together. It's so easy to come into conflict, war, and hate. Because the Ego is empowered and anything under it, anything making you feel powerless, you will with no problem suppress, manipulate, censor, undermine, and delete or kill what needs to be done for your very own survival. As well as for the survival of your tribe, community, and countries with all of their collective ego. Humanity is driven by division, anger, hate, fear, materialism, and most dangerously, ignorance and willful blindness for any action that is decided and taken. This all may have served a hundred years ago, helped evolution rise on industrial technology and modernism. But how about today? Right now? Recently, a different new story has emerged, yet it is not mainstream, and the theory of evolution by Darwin is still being taught at schools today because this new story is challenging and goes against the old power structure. And for that it is being put on the forbidden territory for today's science. As technology is advancing in more modern equipment and studies, so is it affecting medical research. What was not possible hundreds of years ago is today possible, and this is scary as we step from the known into the unknown. But as you have seen up to now, the unknown, the mystical and mysterious even though it is scary, it is exciting at the same time. And because it is so controversial it is no wonder and no surprise that we are going to uncover and unravel this new story. It is possible today to extract ancient DNA fossils and compare them with modern DNA. Which has been done. The latest research done by the Department of Evolutionary Genetics, Max Planck Institute for Evolutionary Anthropology, and various institutes published in 2015 by Kuhlwilm, M., Gronau, I., Hubisz, M. The published paper was about ancient gene flow from early modern humans to Eastern Neanderthals. They have found through the analysis of comparing both genome sequences that between modern human gene flow running into the Altai Neanderthal lineage was pointing towards a correlation of 1.8% in similarities. This means we might have walked on the surface of the earth together with them but did not descend directly from them. The gap between the DNA is far too big to be a direct descendent. This indicates that we showed up on earth, 200 000 years ago based on the new research done on fossils analysis. And as we showed up on earth we already had our advanced and enlarged neocortex and were as modernly advanced as we are today. That goes against any studies about the theory of evolution. The study of genetics goes way beyond just the finding that we did not directly descend from them; but it also points toward something science cannot explain. Science and religion have always been 2 distinct areas where they normally do not merge together, but the discoveries are pointing towards science and spirituality merging together, or maybe I should say, involving intentionality. Before we dive, I need to acknowledge the research I have done. Here is based on Dr. Stephen C. Meyer & physicist Gregg Braden. This makes the entire new story scary, forbidden territory and simply unexplainable, and intriguing… So, when primates' DNA has been studied closely with our modern DNA, it brought us further down the rabbit hole, bringing up other questions and revealing further mysteries that again bring up further other questions...Gorillas, apes, chimpanzees and humans this is where the study starts. Gorillas, apes, and chimpanzees all have the same amount of chromosomes which are 24. While the human is left with 23. Where did that one other go? If we descended from them, right? Here is the intrigue: our human chromosome N2 is an ancient relic of pre-existing other chromosomes found in primates, but the interesting fact is that it has been fused together. In that precise fusion, some functions stayed active, and some were dis-activated but keeping the entire genome intact and perfectly working without damaging it. This is simply indescribable as such sort of fusion cannot be an evolutionary process. It seems like an intelligent design. The fact that some functions were activated and some did not point us in the direction of intentionality. This creation of fusing genes together is a science that involves nuclear fusion, like the power of the sun...we are talking about 200,000 years ago how can this be explained? Going further in this, our chromosome N7, where its FOXP2 gene has linked our jaws, mouths, and brain together, only happened again just in humans. Giving us the ability for complex speech, language and music.

How is it that primates can't sing like us? Not only are we so complex, but only humans have that enlarged neocortex volume, an enlarged brain. We are capable of emotions, sympathy, compassion, and to self-regulate; thanks to the chromosome N2. And this is only accessible to us humans, that level of complexity. One can say that we are over-endowed if we compare ourselves to the animal kingdom. How did this fusion happen can't be explained. The power in these questions is not understanding "the how" but rather diving into the "why". If we are not just here because of some random mutation, that inner intelligence, this intention in us, no matter how it came to be, gives us a new story. It gives us intention. It gives us tremendous power, that we are not here by basic natural process. And if intention is involved, then purpose can be birth out of it. And if some are skeptical, let's just sit in the moment, but what if it was true? What possibilities could we even access? Is it possible that we could, from our own willpower, activate some of these dormant genes? How powerful can a human be, and how come this information is suppressed. Science is now merging with spirituality; this is where the rubber meets the road. This intelligent design is now opening to further questions...who did this? You may call it god, the universe, aliens, whatever you want to call it; there was an intention to give us not only power but also purpose. When we analyze the fundamental laws of our nature, it is based on harmony, cooperation, unity and a participatory role of all engaging with each other. Every little insect and animal has its precise purpose and function, and they communicate together in cycles. Fractal patterns are displayed all throughout the entire universe, up to our molecular strand within our very own DNA. If you look at how birds migrate, they are the information bringers that our weather is changing. Butterflies, insects and bugs help the pollination for the expansion of nature. Every single thing plays a role, needed to adapt and change in order to still be here. Some needed to grow wings to be able to fly, a chameleon needed to be able to change its colors for protection and survival, some needed to grow thicker fur to protect against the cold, and others, such as squirrels, became masters of collecting and building shelter for their own survival. Monkeys have thick, full body hair in order to protect themselves against the filtration of UV sun rays. It all works perfectly in symbiosis. But as we showed up, it seemed we violated theses fundamental laws and simultaneously Darwin's theory at the same time.

We do not have that overall fur and need clothing to protect ourselves from sun, cold, heat, and weather changes. Instead, we have that very complex brain, compassion, and a multitude of dimensions of emotions that no other life form has here on earth. We seem completely out of place and time. Like an ancient artifact found in ancient times in Egypt or Göbekli Tepe not understood with theories and stories flowing and emerging all around. That is so easy; when you think you are just randomly here, you get to survive and destroy all you want, like being stripped away from your true capabilities. But it is time now to write a new story; even if the origin is mystical and scientifically debated, we can start regaining the power of our own being. How incredible can that thought be, the possibility be, that you were not just here because of an evolutionary process that happened to come by chance? Your very existence now has meaning and purpose; it is simply indescribable, which makes it magical. It makes us truly appreciate nature and our environment, how it is interconnected, and that we humans are at a micro level mirroring the macro of the universe. If there is a higher potential, and physics shows this with the many studies in quantum physics, we need to start accessing this potential within us. As our earth, moon, sun, and planets up to the entire galaxy are in a flow of movement, a spin of rotation, we have that same flow of energy circulating within us, flowing, emitting energy inward and outwards. Your thoughts and emotions are not only your compass and internal guidance system, but they also are your tools as to how you energetically emit frequency outward. Energy outward that, in return, influences the fabric of space, time, and matter. The intentions you put outward influence your reality like a radio frequency where you can tune yourself into the channels you desire to see, feel, and experience. You must have played this game once, where you think and search for a red car. Suddenly, all the colors red will appear easy to find, and you will keep seeing red cars everywhere all the time to win the game you are playing. Or you so deeply think about something maybe a place you want to visit, a holiday you dream about. Suddenly, signs will appear all around, like something you see in the newspapers or something you then pick up on the radio or some ad. It really feels like there is a field out there that is interconnected with the thoughts you put out. This shows what in physics they call the quantum field; we can call it tapping into this magic, into this infinite consciousness that connects everything and everyone together, a web of life... How can one still be destructive? If you think about these deep topics, possibilities, and interconnectedness of these actions and reactions or causes and effects, we play a fundamental role in this complex system.

Just as the earth has these gravitational pulls, a dance with the sun and moon and its planets in the solar system, we have that same power as how we pull and attract people into our reality, into our existence. Call it manifestation or the law of attraction, but depending on your vibrational frequency as to your thoughts and emotions, you have the power to magnetize people and situations in your life. Here is where your 7 chakras or energy centers come into play as it is correlated to the 7 laws of the universe, also called the 7 hermetic laws. Here, one can elevate their powers and be aligned with the essence of life itself. Again, we are the only beings on earth capable of doing this. Most other life forms will only exist in the first 3 dimensions of these energy centers. The 3 lower chakras are grounding collecting and survival, then going to the next stage of desires, pleasures, materialism, and reproduction. Finally, as to being stuck in the manipulation, anger, aggression, and ego. But in that last stage, you can integrate and understand your ego and that it can be

213

transformed into the highest forms of creation, willpower, courage, and strength to manifest the life you rightly deserve. The life you imagine for yourself as you embody the essence of your being. You can go back into the chapter on yoga to see the 7 seven chakras in detail, and from the first to last, they intertwine with our universal laws. The seven hermetic laws point to the 1st law being Mentalism, that the All is mind, infinite consciousness. Secondly, the law of Correspondence: as above, so below, from the micro to the macro. The third is the law of Vibration; nothing rests, everything moves, and everything vibrates. The fourth law of Polarity; everything is dual, and opposites are identical in nature but different in degree (I.e., as the fourth law compared to the fourth heart chakras, it's so easy to relate and understand polarities to the heart). Fifth is the law of Rhythm; everything has a pendulum swing, left to right, right to left, and rhythm compensates (I.e., again here in the throat chakra, the rhythm of your speech, how far by your own words can you swing the pendulum as to find compassionate response or deceit, anger, and reactivity). Sixth law of Cause and Effect: all-cause has its effects, there exist many planes of causation, and nothing escapes the law (cause and effect we spoke already in this chapter, and this correlates to the 3rd eye, the sixth chakra; illusions, filters and biased vision and the intuition, wisdom, psychic-powers, mysticism) what you see and perceive with your eye...Finally, the seventh law is the law of Gender. Gender is in everything; all has its masculine and feminine principles on all planes. Here, we talk about the seventh chakra that is connected to the infinite source of consciousness, not the biology of gender itself, which is a different topic. Understanding all these laws possesses the ability to then alchemize and transform their current reality. These are all new emerging possibilities that come with this new story of evolution and the possibilities of what could be achieved here. Evolution means that one is evolving, expanding, and changing, yet this is not possible if we are taught ancient old stories that no longer hold the paradigms. The old story is of competition, and who is the fittest should be revised or least thought as a possibility yet it seems to not be of interest. I don't want to go into conspiracy talk, but I like to compare facts of what is seen against what is revealed or not. In this case it seems any possibilities as to give power and purpose back to humanity is strongly suppressed. But also, merging science with something "intentionally" inexplainable seems way too mystical. Just like how whistleblowers start to come out about

215

corrupt systems or UAP (I.e., Unidentified Aerial Phenomenon), what would be so bad as to let finally the light and truth shine out? It would create new systems. New systems of how we live and create here on earth. The possibility that we are tapping into some of the biggest mysteries is giving us the power to raise our vibration and frequencies. When we start to align with how powerful magical beings we truly are, that we did not emerge just out of chance, there is true wisdom to rediscover within our full potentiality. As we come closer to who we are and what our place is within this construct, we can heal, create, expand, and evolve truly in the evolution of the human species and, in doing so, conjunctively, earth's consciousness. In the end, it all comes up to how you deal with your current reality within your belief systems. If you are in the space of the old story, what you feel, your ego, your emotions feel destructive. In order to release that pressure, you will lash out and might be more aggressive or defensive up to being destructive not only towards yourself but towards others. And that is what we see at the moment with the collective ego; we go into wars, and in politics, we divide and separate. Boundaries and separation form as who is awakened or not, who is dismissive or not, who is a follower, and who is a truth seeker, information or misinformation. It is an entire division coming towards destructive patterns and behaviors. To numb oneself as it gets too much, one will then seek distractions such as binge eating, porn, sex, endless social media scrolling, or hard drugs. All just to escape the mind, to escape the unbearable reality. But there is another way to evolution than being the fittest, the strongest that needs to survive. Dangerously, though, we can also swing the pendulum way far on the other side towards spirituality. But swinging it far too much can also lead to destructive behaviors or ignorance of reality. That can look like using spirituality as an escape from reality. Ignoring one's feelings and emotions by reading more spiritual topics or watching positive videos one after the other. This shadow side of escape can also be called spiritual bypassing. Telling oneself feeling bad is not good, so I will just focus on the good, on the positive. This can look something like pushing other people away from your life because you don't like that "bad vibe" they emit. Surround yourself with only love and positivity, as if you were wearing glasses and are looking at the world through the lens of that colored glass. Telling yourself that is the way to be happy forever, to ignore all the bad stuff, to escape contrast. This is the very myth of our

217

dimensionality is that we will never escape contrast. As much as one wants to avoid, suppress, and ignore, it will always come back to action and reaction; the cause and effect are simply inevitable, and nothing escapes this.

But there is a way, the new emerging story is a way to find meaning and purpose in this existence as in what you want to create. And all starts with these negative thoughts, these emotions, and the divisions we see around us. We have collapsing structures in nature, governments, humanity, earth, education, the medical system, and our children that are the seeds of tomorrow. Whenever an era comes to collapse and shift, it pushes towards birthing something new. Creating new sustainable systems. How much does society and civilization need to be destroyed and recreated again and again in order to finally learn? I believe these times of extremes and separations are inviting us to come close to being in harmony again. The pendulum swing does not need to be swung way too far on the left or on the right. Letting it come to settle in the center is what it means to find balance again within the polarities of our current reality. And this starts by acknowledging that we are part of this complex structure, that we are meant to evolve in harmony not only with each other but with society in general, with nature, with Earth, and the entire Universe at large. And this starts with you. Recognizing the interconnectedness with all that there is. We need to stop pushing our feelings away, our emotions that are bringing us information about our inner compass. The start begins within. And after we start our healing journey, we caretake our abandoned inner child. And as a practice outward, we stop at the same time abandoning other people in judging them and shaming them, for not having the same beliefs. There are ways to find constructive, meaningful, and compassionate conversations instead of pushing one out. A person that is angry, needs to be started, to be approached as someone that is in fear and totally alone. Pushing them away is just the same as pushing yourself away. Like in yoga, when one says Namaste, that is the very meaning of I acknowledge you inside of me. We all mirror each other in some way; we all pull and attract people in our lives to point towards certain aspects within us that need to be addressed and healed at the same time. We all walk each other home to the heart if we let that feeling of fear down and simply surrender to what it currently is. As we start this journey alone and come to meet others, we can create new, meaningful structures. And I want to explain this in that aspect of our relationships, not only to ourselves but towards others and our world at the same time. The dysfunctional adult today comes from a culture and society that has abandoned that little child decades ago. If we want to birth a new society and way of living, we need to address what is currently not going right. This can start with parenting (I.e., shortly seen in the previous chapter). And I mean with this conscious parenting, as what we have been doing for decades is simply dysfunctional and not working anymore with our current reality. I believe this is a major part too within our own evolution. Our children are the future of tomorrow. Especially if you were born after the 80's, these children are called indigo children, crystal children, star-seed children, or light warriors. They came here on earth with very high vibrational frequencies of their own. They are already independent and creative thinkers, highly intuitive and imaginative on their own. Some can recall divinatory dreams (past or future), and others are highly connected to plants and animals. They do not operate well with strict authorities or environments such as school systems or authoritarian rules put on them. They are visionaries, and free thinkers and have a very new liberate way of seeing things. They want to share their absolute truth and sovereignty over their own being. Sadly, our society doesn't understand this, and we stamp them with ADD/ADHD or some kind of label of psychological disorder. Worst of all, medicating them dims the light, gifts, and frequency that they should be sharing with the world. As parents, it is our duty to guide them. We are not meant to be their teachers, but we can learn from them; they chose us as parents, just in the same way that you have chosen your parents as you decided to come here on earth. The shaming, violence, programming, and abandonment absolutely need to stop, and see them as you being their guide and them being your light. We need to recognize the cyclic ways of evolution that have been repeating for thousands of years. The future is created and can only continue existing if we go towards a harmonious and conscious community with unconditional love for each other and for Gaia (I.e., Mother Earth). The change has to start as a recognition, a spark of awakening in your heart then further guided onto the children up to rising the frequency of the collective. As we are coming to the end of this chapter, how does evolution resonate with you? How do you want to live your experience of your limited construct, knowing you are part of a web of creation that has been seeded with intentionality? That we all emanate a frequency of vibration, and we transfer information not only alone but also collectively to remember who we are. Where did we come from, and where are we going? We will dive in depth in the final chapter, but within this process of evolution, we can start to recognize that we are way more than we think. We are way more powerful than one can imagine. That we are not here by chance and that the story needs to be re-written. That change starts with you. By reading this right now, you have received a part of the download; the key has been activated now, but all is up to your free will; what will you choose to do with this information. To the ancient beliefs and the new emerging ones...And yet again, this chapter has brought us a little bit closer to healing, to the recognition of your true power, and that together, we can start to walk the journey towards ending suffering as we integrate polarities. By realizing that all is part of a duality that needed to exist as it is we can see what it means to be one and whole again.

#

Chapter Twelve
Plant Medicine

#

In this chapter on Plant medicine, I want to dive into the activation of our human potential outside of the realm of our known physical construct, culture, society and our medical system. This is about not only finding the path to oneself but also about understanding humanity around us, our relationships with one another, our relationship with the earth, and what mother nature provides. There is so much more in the world of plant medicine I want to share with you and in that matter, I will make this chapter a bit longer than the previous ones. But it's just so important that we come closer to our bodies and back to nature. Shift old narratives and stories and unveil the other side and aspect no one's talking about. Again, here an entire book could be written about plant medicine, but I have picked some of the important ones to me according to my own research. That being said, we will dive into 5- Meo-Dmt, DMT, LSD, Psilocybin, Mescaline, Poppy flower, Kanna, Blue lotus flower, and lastly, Cannabis. Even though Cannabis does not have a psychedelic molecular compound to it, it is still a powerful medicinal plant gifted from nature. In the spectrum of plant medicine, it has various healing properties and consciousness expansion possibilities that we will discuss further in this chapter. In the previous chapter, we have spoken about evolution and how we could reclaim our power within a new emerging story, and here we are not only going back to understanding our power and connection. But we will dive back into our ancestry because plant medicine is something very ancient, thousands of years old, yet we have forgotten about it. Luckily, now it is returning back. We are returning to our roots because the paradigm today is no longer working. If you look at the pharmaceutical industry, their business is flourishing the more one stays sick and dependent on them. That's how they make money. They have no interest in you getting better; as long as you are sick and in need of them, you are a source of income for them. As harsh and as sad as this may seem. This is the harsh reality of the medical business. It's a billion-industry business for the benefit of its shareholders. Secondly, the medicine they produce is already derived from plants, but it will, of course, not just be that; it will include some other chemical cocktail that will make you dependent on them, addicted to them by needing more and more. As you fall into that trap, you become their perfect client. Our physical bodies have such a complex metabolic pathway that there is no other way than the need to write down the side effects. Because everything is so interconnected you cannot treat something by not possibly affecting something else in your body. As we talked about in the chapter on inner biology and sickness, disease doesn't just come like that. It has its energetic roots and causes before it manifests into something physical. And plant medicine can help us not only understand the causes but also treat the ailments at their cause without any of those side effects. Our ancestors used these very gifts of nature, and so we will dive into that ancient magic, these ancient rituals and settings, so that we can find ways to empower ourselves again with nature rather than with the illusions of what the pharmaceutical industries sell us. Plant medicine is a gift of nature, Mother Earth, giving us medicine, healing properties, and relaxants or energizers for hundreds to thousands of years. If you look at the booster coffee or cocoa drink it energizes and revives you mentally and physically, even said to heal the microbiome in the gut...They all come from nature: the cacao tree (Theobroma cacao) or the coffee plant (Coffea arabica). These are plants and trees, among many others, that have healing, grounding, and many more properties found in nature. Tea leaves or flowers are also used in nature for calming, detoxing, de-stressing, or rituals done to invite with an open heart and loving community as the Japanese and many other cultures do. Apart from the healing properties, nature has also given us plant medicine that has psychedelic components. And if we are on a spiritual journey, this is also an important part of it. As many things are being shadow-banned, talked about as negative and destructive by the government and splitting society, it is a pointer for us to want to investigate deeper into the topic. The word psychedelic actually derives from the ancient Greek "psihi" (I.e., soul) and "dilosi" (I.e., manifest), which makes the word soul-manifesting. As we honor the traditions in a sacred setting, we allow and unravel the deepest aspects within us, and by that manifesting, whatever messages need to come through as we connect and download directly from source back into our souls. When we create a setting with candles, or powerful intention, surrounded by nature and the wish to deeply be open to receive, that is what makes the difference between working towards your inner journey of healing compared to something done at a party as recreational abuse. And no wonder that is also where you can have that so-called "bad trip." Therefore, intention, setting, and being surrounded by love, trustworthy people, and like-minded Psychonauts make all the difference in this journey. Since the beginning of this book, we have unraveled healing and deconstruction techniques of how to climb over that mountain of suffering; we are getting closer to our soul and what we internally crave to be able to live that life that is meaningful and purposeful. Like an onion, we peel layers by layers to find that deep core meaning and sense of our existence. This takes tremendous hard work; it takes the daily rituals, the Mala prayers, and the constant inner work to shed light as soon as an emotion or thought rises up, being positive but mostly also negative. The ones that truly hurt and make us question our existence, our daily struggles, our choices, and why we fight the fight we are fighting. Literally called the dark night of the soul because that is what it feels like. When it gets so tremendously hard, you sometimes feel as if you have hit a massive wall. The point of not knowing what to do next. That feeling of being severely stuck. How can you choose yourself without losing them? How can situations or problems unfold for the justice and good of all, where all can find a state of being in a win/win situation instead of that win/lose? How can we stop these coping mechanisms and that constant sacrifice for others meanwhile abandoning ourselves, our self-love, and self-worth in the process for the greater good of others? In following our heart, we can have that feeling of being egoistical if others are affected by our choices. And so, we question how to proceed in that energy flow of uncertainty. There is truth in that behind your expansion and growth; you need to leave sometimes close ones behind so that they can achieve their own growth and expansion instead of being constantly under your "protection". Instead of them being "mothered" or "fathered" by you, you actually avoid their growth. But all these questions can only be answered if you are doing brutal and honest inner work daily. The teachings have been since the beginning of this book; but often life comes in between. We slip into the comfortable routine, and we let go of our daily rituals, programming, and journaling; we slip into that unconscious state. And if one is not rigorous with doing this constant work that is really tough, tiring at some times, and lonely; there is a possibility to get lost again under the surface level of the deep seas of the unconscious waters. How can you heal or change what you do not know if you do not stick to that daily routine of spiritual work?

Well, here is the answer. Psychedelic plant medicine can get you there. It can act as a shortcut if you feel stuck, or it can act as an eye-opener if you fully lose your compass and have no idea how to return back to your spiritual journey.

When we are stuck, and all we see is this physical reality, it seems as if we have a glass ceiling over our heads. We create these constructs and barriers that keep us tied down, that keep us confined in a box. What plant medicine can offer is the expansion of your consciousness way beyond this physical reality. It shatters your seemingly created box, and opens your eyes into an entirely different dimension, a different space reality where you rise higher and see out of an outer world perspective. Your vision and understanding are so clear, it breaks all ancient programming, all ancient beliefs and illusions. These plant medicines have the power to alter your state of consciousness, your perceptions, and, as said, visions of reality. One in particular, called the God Molecule or Spirit Molecule, is one that contains the chemical compound 5-Meo-Dmt. It is scientifically not truly understood how it reacts and interacts; but it seems to bridge connections within our brain synapses that would never happen in a regular normal waking state in the day...The research on this is quite lacking in human studies, scientific studies, and peer-reviewed journals. However, testing on diverse animals has shown powerful modification in innate behavior patterns and promoted structural neural plasticity in mice. For humans, it has always again and again been linked with near-death experiences, Oneness, God, Infinite love, death of the ego, and a state of awakening. What practitioners have experienced, the realms they have been seemed more real than this reality. Which makes us wonder about its other benefits... So, let's dive deeper into the subject: 5-MeO-Dmt (I.e., full name 5-Methoxy-N, N-Dimethyltryptamine) is most often consumed via synthetically produced vapor or smoked but can also be harvested from certain plants, snakes, Colorado River toad (Incilius Alvarius) or the Bufo Alvarius toad from the desert of Sonora, Mexico. Now, mind the stories you might have heard about licking the frog in order to get high; that is not only untrue and irresponsible but is also extremely dangerous. The back of the toad is very toxic and contains a highly poisonous venom; if it is licked directly, it could cause one to eventually end immediately at the ER with cardiac arrest, bacterial tongue infection, or, worst case scenario, physical death, and this is not meant in a metaphorical sense...As explained at the beginning of this chapter, there is a sacred setting, ritual, and order to respect if you want to dive into this journey with love intention, download, and have no unwanted so-called "bad" trips. Such an act, as just previously described, would not only be one of being irresponsible, but at the same time, it would be violating and disrespecting these very gifts of the sacred plants and animals' kingdom provided to us by Mother Nature and Earth. So how is it then consumed? The harvest and process are done by removal of the toxins and then by letting it dry. The dried powder afterward is snuffed or smoked with a ritual of thanks and prayers to the connection with Mother Earth and its gifts, with the intention to reveal, guide, and show us the way. The history of 5- MeO-Dmt dates back thousands of years, as traces of the chemicals, including various other psychoactive plant medicines, were found in an artifact located in the highlands of the southwest Bolivian mountains.

231

Archaeologists found a leather-wrapped bundle of tools for preparing and inhaling snuff. They radiocarbon-dated the bundle to between 905 and 1170 CE (current era), from the Tiwanaku Empire period. Much is unclear about the date, as toads were also depicted in ancient Japanese history as well as in early Dynastic Egypt, roughly 3000 BC (before Christ). Even in India, ancient Sumerian or China where, vases and stone carvings of snakes dated 21st century BC, which opens the debate for the exact origin for the use of medicinal animals but a depiction of close connection of human tradition honoring nature and animals. 5-MeO-Dmt is also called the god molecule or spirit molecule because its effects on the perception of the human consciousness bring you far beyond this 3- dimensional reality. It is known to bring people beyond time, space, and form. It is like leaving the human body, identities, and beliefs to reconnect to something bigger, to the unity and oneness of all. The particularity is that you do not have any visuals, hallucinations, or sounds perceived; it's a powerful journey inwards, accessing your true inner essence, and real death of ego, self-dissolution for 20 min. Many reports of Psychonauts have said that any problems they had before taking 5-Meo were afterward irrelevant. It changes so powerfully your life and perceptions that it treats anxiety, misbeliefs, and illusionary problems. People also reported to have created a shift in their lives by changing their environment, such as jobs, health, relationships, or any unswerving pattern. Connected to their highest frequencies and divinities, after the experience, people knew their mission and purpose in life, and with that vision, they made a shift of 360° and radically changed for the better. 5-Meo is not only smoked or snuffed but can also be taken like a brew or elixir drink, known to be prepared by an Indigenous tribe called the Secoya tribe in the Ecuador region. The Secoya tribe calls the brew Yagé (I.e., spelled yahwué) the primary ingredient of Yagé being 5-Meo. According to the indigenous tribe and traditions, it has been said that the plant knowledge and ingredients were brought to the tribe many thousands of years ago. From the light beings that came down from the stars. They have been told to access this way their highest powers and mystical experiences and give access to different densities of reality. Up to today, 5- Meo is the most powerful, profound, life-changing, and eye-opening psychedelic and has all reason to be called the "God Molecule". Diving now deeper into these plant medicines, there is another chemical compound that is closely related to 5-Meo-Dmt, which is named DMT

(I.e., N, N-Dimethyltryptamine). As we know now, 5-Meo doesn't have visual hallucinogenic effects, but it's a closely related cousin; so to speak, DMT is highly visual. DMT is found in various plants and rainforest trees such as Phalaris, Delosperma cooperi, Acacia, Virola tree, and Chacruna tree, to name a few...It is a hallucinogenic substance found in these various plants and rainforest trees: extracted in the Amazon, Bolivia, Peru, Costa Rica, and Ecuador...to name a few places. It is always used in religious and sacred ceremonies, particularly shaman ceremonies in South America, in order to invoke a state of spiritual enlightenment with visual hallucinations. Not only do they invoke the states of connection, messages, and guidance. But mostly powerful healing and shadow release of trauma by body and mind cleansing through purging. DMT is the main hallucinogen among others in the plant brew Ayahuasca. The brew is sacredly prepared by the ancient Shipibo tribe from the Amazonian rainforest in Peru. These tribes & shamans reported, like the Secoya tribe, to have received the knowledge & preparation from the light beings, also called the star people, that have descended from the stars down to earth to transmit the knowledge. It is known for the brief but intense psychedelic high that comes from consuming it. Which can be taken through smoke, vaping, or, as the tradition found in the Ayahuasca ceremony, taken through the gut by drinking the brewed tea elixir. Its effects are very visual, with strong components in hallucinations and astral travel. Reports of people who have taken Ayahuasca have reported having seen and spoken to a female deity that gave them powerful insight into what they needed to shift and change in their lives. She has been called the mother of nature or the mother ayahuasca. Profound astral travel has also been reported into different realities and worlds that seemed more real than just a dream or hallucination. People returned healed and felt enlightenment from their journey. A powerful connection that they were not separated any longer but more connected with nature and the universe. DMT was first synthesized in 1931 by the British chemist Richard Manske. He discovered that it induced high visuals and sounds. Important to know that these chemicals are found in many various plants and animals in nature but are also produced by humans within the mammalian brain. Up to this date, science still cannot understand why and how DMT is produced but it seems closely related to our pineal gland activating the gamma brain wave. It seems to have the power also to increase our vibrations and frequencies, receive messages, or speak with otherworldly entities such as angels, spirits other beings through telepathic conversations. Quite a mystery because these reports have been compared to other people and case studies, and the similarities of experience are astonishingly and closely the same. Could we have access to a different dimension we still do not understand? As the benefits are so powerfully healing and give so much knowledge; this might be something science is now diving deeper into. Slowly, these chemicals are being released to new perspectives of psychedelic research and healing retreats rather than just being viewed as a drug. In the year 2016, scientists Szabo & Frecska published research in the Institute of Clinical Medicine, Oslo, Norway, and found that DMT produced in the human pineal gland had a protective compound related to treating neuron inflammation and enhancing neuron protection within dying cell tissues that were not enough oxygenated. DMT might be released in the case of low oxygen in the brain and cell tissues. This is what people might experience in near-death experiences or when some are dying and report finally reconnecting to the source and in peace before they go, unscarred and liberated. Another researcher, Stanislav Grov, PHD, proposed that

DMT is released in the pineal gland and could be activated by holotropic Breath-work, a technique of breathing oxygenating the entire system and brain region through controlled hyperventilation. By activating this, we would release serotonin and DMT out of pineal secretion, accessing us humans directly to instant healing, self-regulation, mystical experiences, and powerful states of transcendental meditation by the release of the chemical in our brain and not through the need of taking it externally. As growing interest is emerging in psychedelics, the risk of endangering the species and the Amazonian forest is becoming a threat due to the expanded interest in tourism. Knowing that we can release these chemicals in our brain by ourselves by doing focused meditation on the pineal gland, heart-brain coherence technique, rising with breath work, the kundalini Shakti power (kundalini yoga) or the Holotropic Breath-work is becoming the new solution aside from getting the chemical via synthesized lab production. What is really stunning here is that DMT and Cannabinoids (I.e., what is found in Cannabis) are naturally produced in our brains! We are literally internally wired for this. Alcohol, if you take it, is something totally unknown in our system, a toxic poison. Yet what people so often call "drugs" are being produced in your brain, and your brain holds receptors for it. Try shifting conversations with that! It's just so divine and powerful.

Speaking about powerful conversations and societal movements, we are now going to dive into LSD. In the 60s throughout the 70s, a powerful shift started within the population and culture at large with the LSD and Cannabis movement. An entire movement of awakening happened with an enormous shift in consciousness for Growth, Freedom, and Truth. People shared the vision of peace and love; an entire movement of liberation against war, suppression, and control of the higher authorities over the sovereignty of each individual human being needs to end. That life is so precious, the world is so precious, and the hate, the programming, and war were no longer an option to resolve social, cultural, and injustices in general. In this movement of liberation, people started questioning the narratives that radio, television, and newspapers were broadcasting. Instead of previously, blindly following everything, the questioning became stronger, and the feeling and desire to be free of any illusions became louder. It is no surprise that not long after that, in June 1971, President Nixon declared the "war on drugs". He increased the size and control of federal drug agencies. Everything is being shut down, making all of these eye-opening substances illegal. Taking the control back with governmental rules and regulations. We will circle back on this topic of censorship, cancel culture, and this state of being in or out of the "box" at the end of this chapter. But back to LSD, where does this come from, and how is this a plant? LCD (Lysergic acid diethylamide), its primary ingredient being Lysergic acid, is actually a naturally occurring compound found in Rye seeds. Since this element is natural and not something that is only made in a laboratory, LSD is a chemical compound that has at least some ties to the natural world and is a gift of nature. The psychoactive effects of LSD were firstly discovered in 1943 by Albert Hofmann at Sandoz Labratories, Switzerland. As an experimental drug for psychotherapy and scientific research, it generated widespread interest from the intellectual establishment and was even secretly investigated by the U.S. Central Intelligence Agency (CIA) for potential applications in "mind control" ... The reason for the use of this is that if you have untreated trauma or a kind of brainwashing is done to you, LSD has that specific side effect aspect to augment the psychosis and push towards a bad trip. In the case of a military program that would create a perfect obedient soldier, unquestioning, frustrated or in anger, ready to execute the ordered given mission to get the job done, no questions asked. On the other hand, again, respecting the setting and working towards your healing and awakening journey with gratitude and respect, the powers that LSD can offer and help are mind-blowing and tremendously powerful. Scientific research has found LSD to be an effective treatment of a number of ailments, including alcoholism, addiction, cluster headaches, and anxiety associated with terminal illness. People on assisted therapies have effectively reduced, to even stop, the various addictions they were dealing with. This was reported after the first or second trials. They felt at ease, happy, grounded, no more fears. This helped to open the doors towards the beauty and reality of the world, which they were now seeing from a higher and broader perspective. This was the key to finally letting go of the old unwanted patterns and finally healing mentally. The consumption of LSD is associated with mystical experiences that may facilitate self-reflection and personal growth. It has been called the first modern entheogen, a group that is otherwise limited to traditional plant preparations or extracts. In treating pain, it can greatly reduce or distort the perception of pain. This is likely due to a variety of factors, as the hallucinogenic effects allow the pain to be interpreted as a different sensation (i.e., a tickling sensation from a painful stimulus) and also possess potent anti-inflammatory properties that likely contribute to this effect. As a final summary about LSD, from the effective treatment of ailments to the blend of its mind-altering effect on consciousness and visual hallucination, have proven to have adverse effects such as visual geometry, hallucinatory states, time distortion, enhanced introspection, conceptual thinking, increased music appreciation, euphoria, and ego loss. The visual geometric pattern mostly bridged the understanding of interconnectedness with the nature surrounding us.

The next interesting topic is now Psilocybin (I.e., more commonly known as mushrooms). Psilocybin is a naturally occurring psychedelic compound produced by more than 200 species of fungi and the effects of some plants and fungi have been known and deliberately exploited by humans for thousands of years. The earliest evidence of magic mushroom use is a mural that was found in Northern Australia which depicts mushrooms and psychedelic illustrations. Archeologists have dated it back to 10,000 BCE. Rock paintings in Spain suggest magic mushrooms were around prehistoric people in Europe in 4,000 BCE (before the current era). Studies in research started only later in the 1990s at the University of Zurich; this was one of the first studies after the previously discussed government ban in 1971 (the act of war on drugs). They seem to have found a link that psilocybin increases brain activity but also the treatment of numerous psychological conditions and chronic pain. Also, visual perception and the altered state of consciousness seem to bridge an unexplainable phenomenon reported by the users in the study. It helps strongly against addictions and cravings; various studies and reports present a number that 80% of participants were instantly no longer in need of their cravings after being asked 16 months later, after the initial period start of the psilocybin trial. In addition to treating addictions successfully, astonishing results were also shown on anxiety, depression, post-traumatic stress disorder, hopelessness, and loss of purpose and meaning in life. People felt a connection to their higher self; this was acute and long-term observed from; Researchers James E., Robertshaw T.L., Hoskins M., and Sessa B. A study–trial experiment on psilocybin at Human Psychopharmacology Clinique. The study brought up positive changes in personality and increased altruism, Enhanced feelings of connectedness, and Ego dissolution. Reduction of egotistical attitudes and narcissism and induced greater prosocial behavior, substantial decreases in depressive and anxious symptoms persisting up to 6 months after a single active treatment. In another study, participants report positive persisting effects in areas of mood, behavior, and attitudes up to 14 months after psilocybin therapy. Increased meditation depth, Increased incidence of positive self-dissolution. Patients talked about Bliss, heaven, Nirvana, "Major shift in attention and perspective of the world", "Clarity", Unity consciousness and ego dissolution, "Greater understanding of self", "Persisting feeling of self-awareness and insight", "Feeling more "grounded", "Access to deeper parts of oneself". It seems there is a link and connection with the brain synapses, and it's still a mystery and not well understood. But life changing claims from the patients for sure. Since then, in Europe, some states in the US are slowly opening facilities (I.e., Psilocybin retreats) under medical and psychological surveillance, with the honoring of sacred sessions of discussions and integration. To me a huge leap to what humanity has been through since then.

Diving deeper into our plant medicine explorations, we are now opening the subject of Mescaline (3,4,5 trimethoxyphenethylamine).

Mescaline is a naturally occurring psychedelic proto-alkaloid of the substituted phenethylamine class, known for its hallucinogenic effects comparable to those of LSD and Psilocybin. It occurs naturally in the San Pedro cactus, the Peruvian torch, the Bolivian torch cactus, the peyote cactus, and other species of cacti. It is also found in small amounts in certain members of the bean family, Fabaceae, including Acacia berlandieri. Peyote has been used for at least 5,700 years by the Native Americans in Mexico for its healing medicinal properties. Mescaline has a wide array of suggested medical usage, including treatment of alcoholism and depression, due to these disorders having links to serotonin deficiencies. It induces a psychedelic state similar to those produced by LSD and psilocybin but with unique characteristics. Subjective effects may include altered thinking processes, an altered sense of time, and self-awareness, with closed- and open-eye visual phenomena. The prominence of color is distinctive, appearing brilliant and intense. Recurring visual patterns observed during the mescaline experience include stripes, checkerboards, angular spikes, multicolor dots, and very simple fractals that turn very complex. Like LSD, mescaline induces distortions of form and kaleidoscopic experiences, but they manifest more clearly with eyes closed and under low lighting conditions. Findings indicate that mescaline in any form may produce a psychedelic experience that is associated with spiritual significance and improvements in mental health with no potential for abuse or addiction. Many reports have been done since studies done on mescaline, and it has proven not only to have helped people with depression, anxiety, and co-dependence, but people have found their spiritual path, forgiven past traumas, and reconnected with love for themselves and their love, for life at all Levels.

Now let's discuss the very controversial topic of Opium (Poppy flower). This is a sacred flower of nature, but you will understand why it has been misused. A Gift from the Buddhist Monastery: Buddhist Medical Practices in the Assimilation of the Opium Poppy in Chinese Medicine during the Song Dynasty (960–1279). Opium is not as taught originating out of ancient Chinese medicine but rather gifted to them by Indian Buddhist monks, as listed above. The scripture found about opium poppy in the Song dynasty, Kaibao bench, published in 974, stated that it is prescribed for improving the circulation of qi (life force or, in yogic traditions, "Prana") and reducing fever. It cures nausea, phlegm in the chest, and cinnabar poisoning. It is said that it can be cooked with bamboo juice to make porridge. It is a cold medicine and very good for the intestines. Gradually, the plant medicine later evolved to treat diarrhea, coughing, and spams. Here is where the violation of this sacred plant occurred as it was taken into a lab for further scientific and medical studies for pharmaceutical purposes. It was only in 1903 that an alkaloid was isolated from opium to obtain morphium (pain killer) and heroin, which then pushed the medicinal properties to become more of a drug, leading to addictions. Sadly, that was never the purpose of this plant in its original form, and it did not induce these addictions. It originally treated stomach issues among various ailments previously listed. The obtained oil from the opium poppy plant seeds was also used for medicine purposes as it contains a fair rich amount of lecithin. This phosphorus-rich substance is recommended to reduce the bad cholesterol in the blood and improve the nervous system's functions. To summarize, opium is a powerful plant medicine used by ancient Sumerians 5000 years ago, powerfully supporting and healing before it started to be synthesized, chemically modified, and isolated to create abuse in the early stages of modern times and the early Industrial

Revolution. For the pharmaceutical industry, a new step into the creation of addiction is to then be at the forefront of now to be able to "treat" addictions. For the beautiful ancient story and traditions of the poppy flower, a distant remembrance of what it once was. Nature's given plant medicine. Another flower that nature gifted us is Sceletium Tortuosum (also called Kanna). This beautiful flower grows and has been cultivated in South Africa for hundreds of years by hunters and gatherers. The contained alkaloids – especially mesembrine and mesembrenone – cause psychoactive effects by binding to the serotonin receptors of our nervous system. Because of the serotonin bind, Kanna acts as a natural antidepressant. It improves mood and relieves stress, tension, and anxiety. Because this acts in a natural way, you don't have any side effects or addictions compared to traditional pharmaceutical drugs like the use of Prozac, Valium, Xanax, or Lysanxia, to name a few among the most sold antidepressants worldwide. With natural plants, Individuals become friendlier and more open, so it's easy for them to socialize and communicate instead of chemical drugs. These drugs often leave you with brain fog, trouble concentrating, lack of appetite, and the saddest part of all, loss of interest and pleasure in life; up to long-term use could drive you to suicidal thoughts; all that you would avoid by using natural plant medicine such as Kanna. Kanna's euphoric effects are also suitable for relaxation. Recent studies confirm the positive effects on concentration and attention. Used as part of spiritual rituals for the South Africans, this plant has won its place in traditional healing circles. Kanna can be snuffed, smoked, vaped, or used in teas.

Staying in the flower plant medicine given by nature, we are now diving into the final two plants of this chapter, the Blue Lotus flower and Cannabis. The blue lotus flower (Nymphaea caerulea) the ancient Egyptians called the sacred flower. Carvings of this flower can still be found today in their temples, carved in the stones to honor traditions and its sacredness. Growing by the banks of the river Nile, this sacred plant was used by the Egyptians in ancient times (estimated c. 3200 BC- AD 400). It was prized for its beauty, symbolism, and for its consciousness-altering effects. But it's powerful healing powers are also to consider. Scattered petals were found in the tomb of Pharaoh Tutankhamen; researchers and archaeologists thought that these flowers were purely symbolic. However, there is a growing body of research that is pointing towards the Egyptians using Nymphaea caerulea to induce ecstatic states, euphoria, and visions. This made them want to dive deeper into this flower and its properties...Nymphaea caerulea contains the alkaloids apomorphine and nuciferine. Apomorphine acts as a potent, direct, and broad-spectrum dopamine agonist activating all dopamine receptor subtypes. This is a direct reason why it is used to treat Parkinson's disease, but also because of some sedative effects, it has been broadly used in a variety of psychiatric conditions, such as mania, hysteria, schizophrenic excitement, anxiety, dementia, and most importantly, alcohol-related disorders. On the other hand, its second compound, Nuciferine, was found to be effective for anti-tumor and anti-viral properties. Because it has anticoagulant properties as well, it has a strong effect on lowering blood pressure and weight loss, adjusting blood lipids, lower blood cholesterol, treating fatty liver, and promoting blood circulation. Both properties balanced perfectly contribute to a variety of medical conditions that can be treated; especially for the human psyche, such as the mind. Nuciferine's ability to penetrate the blood-brain barrier makes it an interesting candidate for treating diseases of the brain. But also to open the doors of being fully conscious, altering reality (without any visual effects) perception, and powerfully bringing one back to the present moment. A perfect tool for meditation for those with concentration problems, as the effects of drinking it in tea alter perception and mindfulness, bringing you constantly to be fully present and to quiet the mind. All thoughts seem to be inaccessible as you just observe the now in silence and stay present. As if you were seeing the world for the first time...Ancient traditions said, the use of this flower was done by soaking it in their wine for several weeks to induce more powerful effects.

Last but not least, let's talk about Cannabis as we now approach the end of this chapter. As discussed in the beginning of the chapter, Cannabis doesn't carry any psychedelic compound to itself. It has tremendous medical properties, yet it has been shamed by society and culture at large, and in general, it has been labeled as a recreational drug. One of the most popular and oldest plant medicines known for millennia and dates as far back as 2800 BC. Healing property and use of the plant were found in various ancient texts from the Sumerians, Indian Hindus, Assyrians, Greeks, and Romans, to some appearance in the book of Enoch scriptures from the bibles old Testaments found in the Dead Sea Scrolls, relating it closely to the tree of life in ancient scriptures. Two components found in the plant are THC and CBD. The ratio between CBD and THC makes the medicinal usage more specified; while THC can relax a mind to calm one down, it can also drive you to activate creativity and motivation, which is what is used in the common language of being in a high (Sativa dominant strain) or a low (Indica dominant) state of being. The healing benefits are vast and various and cover a large part of human ailments such as relief of chronic pain, improvement of lung capacity, weight regulation and prevent diabetes, fight cancer, treat depression, mood calming improvement shown in autism, regulate seizures, mend bones, helps in ADD and ADHD (focus, concentration, hyperactivity, cognitive behavior problems), glaucoma treatment, alleviates anxiety, slower down the development of Alzheimer's disease, lower inflammation, help against arthritis pain, helps PTSD (post-traumatic stress disorder) symptoms, relieve with multiple sclerosis, reduce effects linked to hepatitis C while increase effectiveness of treatment, treat inflammatory bowel disease, digestion issues in the gut related to food allergies or intolerances (constipation, diarrhea or acid reflux is all healed powerfully), helps with tremors of Parkinson and finally helps to get away from addictive substances such as alcohol or other various drugs. Strains like Blueberry Diesel, Northern Lights, and Blackberry Kush are the best pick in cannabis strains for cancer treatment as they remedy pain, curb nausea, encourage appetite, and fight depression and fatigue related to the chemotherapy. Strains such as Shapeshifter Sativa, Socal Master Kush, Oregon Lemons Hybrid, Blue Dream Sativa Hybrid, and White Buffalo Sativa are the top five examples to go to for meditation or the expansion of your consciousness. While the body is in a fully relaxed state, the mind can be used to focus powerfully on your desire to heal (visual inner meditation), up to problem solving as to see and think with clarity and spaciousness of your entire being. It activates other portals and inner wisdom while connections are being bridged in the brain. If we take into perspective all of the benefits from a medicinal point of view, it makes sense why this is seen as a drug and has such a bad name; Pharma industries would need to come with ten different medicines a day compared to one tiny plant with all its combined super powerful natural remedies. And not to forget, these plants grow trees in an enormous fast way, making this a very nature-friendly compound and sustainable for the use of wood, furniture, or hemp clothing and fabric tissues (linen, bags, etc.). No more destruction of the Amazonian rainforest (which I'm guessing will not make big industrial companies happy either). Even environmentally speaking, it's a big winner, yet so much is being put into demonizing the plant. The usage goes from smoking, vaping, oil extraction, infused in teas, or as edibles in baking, cookies, or even seeds sprouted on a salad or breakfast porridge as a superfood!

Psychedelics have the power to bring all humanity together, to open their eyes, the realization of being systematically lied to, being programmed and blinded into a so-called "matrix," or to not step "out of the line," or "out of the box". The power of the inner deconstruction of your deepest shadows, programming, and limiting beliefs is lifted and seen unfiltered by plant medicine and spiritual work. Our governmental system encourages alcohol, drugs, over-the-counter medicine, and antidepressants, destroying the proper function of your system along with so many unknown side effects. As if keeping you asleep, drugged like a zombie is easier for "them", or maybe for the serving companies into manipulating people (I.e., their clients). Probably, if we think about all of the properties, healing, and spiritual benefits taken out of this chapter, it is just the fact that a sick and depressed patient is more valuable than a healthy, awakened one. Of course, there will be many layers of awakening each time on the journey, and it might take more than just one try, but the more you walk the path, the more is revealed. There lies within you so much strength, power, and potential. Your path until now the struggles and challenges you needed to put yourself through are all part of the process. The spiritual path is a lifetime journey, and so are its gifts and use of plant medicine. But the more you integrate and awaken to your highest, fullest Meta-human potential, the more you can rise and be expanded on a metaphysical level. The final thought about psychedelics and plant medicine, in general, is that it's a bridge to help you expand your consciousness into realization and reveal certain parts and aspects of your entire Reality, the entire meaning of the complex mechanism of the Universe, to finally revealing who You are and the meaning or reason of your existence, which bring us to the last piece down this road. As we have walked together through the various techniques, rituals, and insights, that is where we are now heading up next into the final chapter of this healing, transforming, and awakening journey.

#

Chapter Thirteen
Who am I, why am I here?

#

This is the famous question many philosophers, scientists, thinkers, and visionaries have pondered: who am I, why am I here, and where am I going? But even the saddest, lost, or depressed person might have asked him or herself that same question. We are still that angry person; we are still that person seeking healing and understanding; we are still that one in the rat race or survival mode. Up to this point, you understand now how science and spirituality merge together, how vibrations and frequencies create attractions, synchronicities, and magnetizations, but still, in the midst of daily life, we still cannot fathom and connect the dots. But before we can go to the deep core of the question; I will touch on a few various subjects first before we circle back to that question. You can imagine this like a walk through the woods, with many roads we will take. Hills and lakes, we will pass, paths and mountains we will walk and climb. There will be a lot to unpack, and this final journey will be like a deep dive into the deepest roots of a tree planted in the soil, up to its highest little bud flower seeking sunlight and how it communicated below the surface with the other plants and the inner-net of nature; in order to do so...

When you look at your life right now, you may be dealing with hard things, difficult struggles, and burdens you carry on your shoulders. Whether it is in family dynamics, at work, relationships in general, or even with yourself seeking meaning, belonging, or purpose in your life. Sometimes, the heaviness seems so unfair that it makes you start to state and wonder that you clearly did not sign up for this. But hang on; yes, in a way, you kind of did... As crazy or unfathomable as that may sound. And we can shout at the Universe, God, or how you may want to name it, "It's ok, I got the lesson, I understood, WE understood"! Yet life or situations will throw again and again a curve ball right on to your lap. But as I said, yes you did sign up for this. In your deepest struggles, anger, or fears lies actually tremendous information. As you know by now vibrations attract each other's or polarizations. As long as you don't recognize that pattern and rise into a different state of frequency, you will keep turning around and round. We saw this already in the previous chapters. And this is where ancestral generational healing comes into play. You may have looked by now at your parents, culture and society. But I want you to zoom out a little more. And a little more. Can you look at your bloodline lineage? Can you go as far as you can, see your ancestors from both your parents' sides, and analyze what has been happening there? To give you an example, I can give you a personal glimpse into my ancestral lineage. This will help you understand the exercise I'm trying to convey. I'm a Filipino from my mother's side and Portuguese from my father. Now, if I analyze as far as I can from my mother's side, there has been a generational pattern of slavery, coping, complying, sacrificing, and giving way to others. This can go as far back as the Philippines was attacked and colonized by the Spanish in the period of 1565 and then again in 1898 by the American colonial period and this lasted until 1946. Before being independent and free again. That's more than 300 years of being undermined before going under revolutions, battles, and negotiations to reclaim independence. Wars and colonization came and went, involving many countries among Portugal as well. Which makes this a paradox, this being my other half in my blood-line. If I analyze the Portuguese or Spanish countries, hundreds of years ago, they were the so-called conquistador (I.e., the ones that invaded and conquered). Quite an interesting dynamic, right? But diving that far, I know that some of that information, the Indigenous tribes, and war battles, still runs in my genetic code. Where I can understand how I can be torn between these two very strong and different poles. Talking about ancestry lineage does not mean you have to heal them; we have enough healing ourselves in the here and now, right? But diving that deep and that far, I can maybe find some deep pattern in me about an old ancient part complying, fearful, and sacrificing, and another part wanting to manipulate, bulldoze, and be very egotistical rather than finding the balance and justice in ways of being more compassionate, understanding and find mediation so that every party wins. Looking at my life today, I can completely understand how I could have chosen my family lineage. In that choice, I can see the lessons and teachings in the pain, the struggle, and any past curve ball life had ever thrown at me. So, I now want you to analyze as far as you can go, can you find now a broader and clearer perspective? For example, if you came on earth as an orphan, grew up in different homes and families, and experienced and went through abandonment, only then can you understand the connection, family (blood-related or not), and belonging. So, it goes for all experiences and transformations in life. Diving into ancient ancestral lineages gives us really an immense expansion of how we relate in our day to day, the choices we make, and the struggles we feel deep within. This is all so connected which I will explain further down as we walk this last chapter together...Earth (I.e., 3rd dimension or density) is a place where polarities exist, and exactly mainly for that fact that we can experience anything here; souls that do decide to come here are to experience life's "attractions" among the many rides that can be taken in this "Disneyland park" of this particular galaxy. That being said, we do have other dimensions (I.e., 12 in total) where different points of experience can be done and chosen from; this information came to me as I have downloaded from source in various deep meditations and plant medicine throughout decades of practice and questioning. The 1st plane of density (I.e., 1D) being of crystals and stone minerals carrying in them all frequencies and download information, but they did not develop that awareness of an "I" or the "I am" perspective. They are more like an interconnected "web". The second plane of density (2D) includes some insects and animals; some animals shift between 2D and 3D, like a dog f.ex. that interacts with a human or interactions between 2D and 3D; they have that awareness of a state of being, but not at the level of an "I am". 3D is then our said physical human experience, where there is a recognition of an I, level of ego, time-space reality construct, and polarity (negative and positive / high-low /good and bad, etc...). There is a funny twist here because this level is also the one where the "I" decides to forget in order to experience. As I said, I call it Disneyland, but it has also been called the "blue pearl" by other beings and attracts many to come here because of all the downloaded and left information here on earth. A place to experience the most dense physical matter. Moving on with the densities we have 4D. Which can be seen or perceived as a connecting bridge. This is a shift in consciousness as you realize there is more than just the perceived physical reality; you start to see the mystical interconnectedness. You feel the energies and frequency, and you see the non-physical perceivable. 5D is where no time and space exist. The laws within the fourth density manifestation are much more powerful and direct. Where you can instantly manifest go back and shift to re-create.

You do still have a body, but it is less dense, and you not only remember the Akashic-Records (I.e., an immense library of all created knowledge that was, is, and to be). You remember a story of the past even though you are in a dimension where time and space are an illusion. All happens simultaneously at your own choice of points of experience. The 6th density has no gravity, thought response appears to an energetic level; even at your will and choice, you still can go to the fifth density and manifest a body or travel in other realities using a physical light body. The seventh density is frequency and vibration, but not only that. It is a co-creator of a collective consciousness; planet Earth or mother Gaia is a seven-density being. 8D is pure energy. At this point, there is no longer a form or body; it's a state of energy. In the ninth, density is what you perceive as light. A manifestation of source fragments in a light form. Tenth density is the split in polarities. The point of division, or dividing in order to experience or expand. The eleventh density is the place where the thought is thought, the self-questioning of: who am I? And at the twelfth density is the Oneness. But before the end of this chapter we will circulate back into the 12th density or dimension. This information about the dimensions where important because, in this new age, you hear a lot of talk about 3D, etc... but in the end, this all circles back into such clarity when we start to connect the dots.

First and foremost, you are in this body; as you read about the dimensions, you probably might have thought what does this serve me? I am a human, physical, with all the stuff that comes with being a human, right? But I wanted to talk about the dimensions to give you a deeper sense of perspectives. Because inside your body is some magic, we can even say universal. And for that let's go in the spectrum of science and its atoms at the quantum level. If you were to zoom in at the tiny, tiniest subatomic particle at the plank scale level, you would find protons within atoms that appear to have the same mass as the universe. This quantum calculation is based on Nassim Haramein, who studied physics and mathematics for more than 30 years. As your body cells micro zoomed have protons in it; one could say that the mass of the universe is in each of your cells. This makes us quantum entangled with all the information of the universe. And this could be seen as us humans being a conduit for the universe. Making us ultimately interconnected everywhere at all possible times. Of course, this is just theories and calculations, we could believe this or not. But having science pointing towards some unification is similar to the oneness we hear around spiritual circles nowadays, which makes this a nice merge. The teachings of Haramein also seem very controversial if you research him, but just like in the chapter on evolution, when I hear controversy or even conspiracy, that's when I feel more motivated to research, understand, and find where we could look or relate more deeply into these stories. In our times today, it seems as if more separation is being pushed. Rather than a narrative of oneness. It's always somewhere "us" against "them". This can be seen in politics, in wars, and even in the recent pandemic of the coronavirus. The ones for vaccines and the ones against it. It seems as if we have that need to search who is the bad one, and who is the savior. Which camps are we to position ourselves in? But analyzing this even more closely, it sadly created separated camps and groups fighting with each other, searching for the "devil" in the other. I can, from a lower perspective, understand how it may feel good because wherever camp you stand, you are included, loved, and are in a community of like-minded people. But can we see that this dynamic has been pushing humanity away from each other for thousands of years already? As we have seen in the previous chapters, I want to make you aware of returning back to nature, to our hearts, to love, to finding peace and "ending" suffering, but not as really ending suffering, in a world of polarity and dualities we always will feel some waves of pain or uncomfortable situations; but we might learn how to surf on that wave of "suffering" rather than being crushed by it. Yet, still, we won't take care of this garden if we do not see sacredness in it. That's the same thing happening with Earth right now and all of its divided aspects. The divided aspects are equally the same within you. The fragments of our psyche, the self-hate, and the divisions inside us are just a reflection at a large scale of what is happening around us. Healing aspects within us will heal aspects around us as well. What we see around us are just perceptions and aspects of what we perceive from inward to outward with our consciousness. Consciousness in and of itself is the key to understanding life and how all is intertwined and interconnected. We need to heal the aspects of ourselves first in order to understand and grasp what is going on around us. Use little rituals daily from the examples in this book, and stop pushing away the innate parts of us that make us us. We have been diving so deep into reclaiming our powers, our healing but none of that makes sense if we don't understand the game of this life. Your body is your temple, first and foremost. And if we acknowledge its sacredness its inner magic, functioning and working for us, we can start treating ourselves differently. Talk to ourselves in a different way, in a more loving and compassionate way. If someone is physically ill or mentally down, there is no space to see the broader perspective. We stay locked in our minds, ancient beliefs that life is just randomly happening to you. Circumstances you can't avoid anyway and so we fall into this victimized mentality, this way of being powerless. And when you are in that closed state, it's easy to get manipulated and then swing the pendulum into fear and anger. The aggressiveness and separation we see so much around us is only because there is a lack of love and understanding. But the moment we understand, we can find compassion and start to see our body differently, our health differently, and at that same time, the world around us differently. In this time of extremes, we are being called into change and recognition. As you know by now, cycles will only repeat, and we will only go into a reset again. Just as many have gone before us, just as many civilizations needed to rebuild from scratch. You are here and now in this lifetime. This life you get to experience will only come once in this lifetime in your physical form and family. So, look at your life right now; how are your choices? Your lifestyle? Are you operating out of a state of fear and sacrifice, or are you consciously choosing your story? And these questions are the reason I wanted to dive into the aspect of your ancestors. Why did you choose them? And what can you learn from them? And because I keep saying you chose them, I will explain to you why there is a choice in the first place. Life is a choice. We are always being called into coming back in alignment. Your soul your heart knows best, but our conditioned mind mixed up with cultures and beliefs leave us astray. Look at all the religions; they all bring their hands back to the heart. Christians who do the sign of the cross always end up having palms together by the heart. Hawaiian tribes and indigenous cultures place their palms back into the heart. This points to something within, something inside, like the chakras or energy centers all are aligned following the spine going upward, following an inner essence within. When we quieten enough the mind and the thoughts and bring the awareness within, it's as if we were connecting to an internal intelligence. A form of wisdom of insight, intuition that seems to communicate to us when we dare to listen and trust that inner voice. This connection, this source inside you, is the bridge from the physical to the mystical. From

266

the seen towards the unseen. And this deep connection is what is keeping you alive here on earth in the physical. Let me put it this way: the essence within you is aligned with your physical body. Your physical, astral, and spiritual body are all merged together, and the essence, that inner light, is right at the center of your heart. Like an anchor that uses the physical body to be piloted, to be guided as a sacred vessel. Your body as that sacred temple can be seen as your sacred avatar here on earth. I want to give you an example to grasp this entire concept as words are making this difficult to explain. Your physical body and your inner essence are connected by a silver soul thread. Let's say you are following your dreams, then both physical and mystical are merged, and the soul thread is close up to being fully connected to the heart and fully aligned and merged to its center. But the more you step out of alignment, the more you stray away from your heart's desire; the more distance is being created in this soul thread. When this distance is created, you feel sad, upset, and unfulfilled. The more the distance is created, the more the soul thread is being pulled and stretched into tension. Now, the feeling gets more and more intense and gives rise to anger, disappointment, rage, unheard, danger, and unpredictable state of emotions. The further again it is being stretched, the more one starts to feel totally abandoned, misunderstood, totally alone, and hopeless. At this point, the thread is so far from the heart, so thin, so fragile, that the calling towards the heart is no longer a sound to hear; the inner voice seems silenced. At this very deepest rock bottom point of depression, it seems like the only way out of hell is to die. This would be the only way of reuniting the physical with the essence by death, by breakage of the soul thread; the contract is now torn. The agreement between both are no longer aligned, and so the only way to reunite them is to start over. Moreover, the silver lining in this soul thread is at the pinnacle: The Ego death. This is the sweet surrender of acceptance. To allow to just be. With no name, no thought, no space, no time, nobody. Just like in quantum mechanics the moment of collapse of the wave function, where its state can be anything until it has been observed by consciousness. The death or dissolutions of the ego, in the most horrific experience, can give space to emergence, to the way back to the heart, back into Love, the deepest, most infinite form of Love that you came here to taste. It is the call to oneness and the highest, most direct way to awaken, heal, and shed the old self with all the weight and burden of not being enough for this world.

To wrap this segment up, we are always being called by ourselves to return to the heart. And this brings us to the next understanding of relationships and your highest self. Relationships here on earth are truly the catalyst for understanding, transformation, and expansion. It's in relationships with others, that you discover hidden parts in you. This is where we shed the light on the darkest parts that were unknown. Here is where we grow together and where we also learn how to let go. We attract one another because of matching frequencies because in these frequencies and vibrations, there are lessons and growth to be learned from both sides. This is very important to know because we do hear in a lot of circles to push people away or push the negative out of your life. I just can't agree directly with this. If we are on this path of seeking to understand ourselves we need to understand the other fully as well, and so pushing one away is not what you need to do, or at least not immediately, if I may put it this way. There is a gold nugget in the pain or uncomfortable people we attract into our lives; as they shine the light towards what needs to be healed inward within us, we can understand why they even entered our lives in the first place. If you had pushed them right away, you would have lost this valuable information. We want to collect the most data possible here. When we are face to face with our pain the discomfort, we are facing valuable information of our personal boundaries. This is a gift because without that pain happening, you would not even notice it; this may have stayed buried in your subconscious. When you can start to be grateful for that negative person, for that person that hurt you, you can now consciously choose to let them go. To release them. By releasing them, you need to undergo first the "awakening" of that dormant boundary you had; with conscious conversations, you accept them, see them, hear them validate them fully. If the other person does the same with you, this is a powerful opportunity where you can both grow together. Maybe, in this case, you don't need to go part ways. But if you have learned the lesson, you evolved, and conversations were done fully from the heart with compassion, yet the other person stays stagnant, this is your key moment to leave. In this conscious uncoupling, remind yourself to be grateful for the valuable insights you have gained and that you can bring forward into the next coming relationships. But also, I need to make this clear: leaving with gratitude and love is going to force them to find their own growth and healing. That is their burden to carry, their healing journey, and not yours. In leaving them, they now have the chance to awaken themselves if they were deluded in unconscious behaviors of just relying on you being their "life-vest." ... When I talk about relationships here, I mean this in general, whether in romantic ones, family, work, or friendships; this is for any possible human-to-human interactions we encounter in this lifetime. We are trying to understand why we are here, and this is one of the aspects: remembering the dormant parts, remembering these pieces of gold that are hidden deep down under the surface of what can only be seen by the eye. The more you unravel, to more veils fall off, and the closer you get to your highest self. But what is that highest self? This is not something in you but is actually what makes you "you". Many philosophers have pondered since then about the highest self, but one of the very first that coined that term goes as far back as 18 hundred 1889, more specifically by Blavatsky Helena. Her books and philosophy got me interested many decades ago because Einstein quoted her as being one of his favorite authors. If you research this deeply, it explains it as being the God above us, which can be found in many religions, esoteric circles, or new age. But as I said, I see this more as an essence that makes you. Part of my research, deconstructions, and teachings have always revolved around diving into our own powers and our own possibilities. For that, it may sound triggering to other belief systems, but how could we relate to the approach of a higher power that has a hand above us? This just seems like taking our own power away from being under another hierarchical system, even if this is a spiritual one. This highest-self, I want you to consider it being the possibility of; being an essence of what makes you. That voice guides your choices for your call to be true and self-serving you. Not in a narcissistic or egoistical approach but in the sense of you including everything in existence around you, interacting with you. In a compassionate form of the highest Love for you and them, and "it" at the same time. If we are really connected to one another to all existing things in life, we circle back into oneness, into that singularity before the big bang. Your life, up to this very day, is made of each of the choices you have ever made or will ever make. At this highest level, even at one of the different dimensions or densities, they are in existence. The very key essence is consciousness. Some may have called this as being the god mind or the collective mind. We are searching to know ourselves, but how about this mind searching to know itself... And both zoomed out in perspective being the very same thing. A paradox within the infinite thought. I think therefore I am, or I am therefore I think. For one to know oneself, one needs polarity, an "other", a split in consciousness. The 11th density is the result of that questioning to then at a level below the intention and the need to split itself in order to discover who it is, what it is, what it could do, what it could experience, and how it could expand. Because before the split, before this primary thought or question of "who am I" was the 12th density, the Oneness, the pure infinite source consciousness. The infinite source of consciousness, that was always there and has always been there. But when you have infinity available to you, what would you do? In this infinite space of Love, what is there to experience? To know? If all there is, it just is. Everything in existence is a figment of this infinite consciousness. And you are asking the very same question: who are you, where did you come from, and where are you going? Points exactly back to this question. You are the infinite source of consciousness. This is the same paradox pointing back to its tail. The god's mind is you, and you are it. Your soul is infinite; you decided to come here on earth because of what contracts you did with yourself in order to play a game of what you could possibly experience here. Your existence is infinite; you want

273

to know more about yourself; you decide to come on earth to expand. When your physical body dies, you go back to the source (I.e., yourself), and you gain a bit more knowledge and experience. All the people on earth, all the souls, are doing exactly that; we all gather information, experience, and expansion to know ourselves better and give the information back to ourselves. We can even take this as far as a video game, where you could have many avatars to play the game; you can become poor rich play at different types of players and levels. You can even play in different worlds or upgrade to different magical powers. The end game is to have fun, gather experience, and expand. You are infinite, so what else is there to do but experience what you could do? Therefore, you give yourself this limitation; you give yourself a finite amount of time of a human life span or an animal or a plant. Now, you can play, try different games, and come back again in different forms with different experiences. To put it in another way, the sun is one star, but it radiates many rays, yet all the rays come from that ONE same sun. You are that ray of sun that shines on earth, just as the many other sun rays all being part of that same sun. You are that drop of water, just like the many other drops of water that form that one and same deep ocean.

The drops of water could never be seen as separated, nor the many streams of rivers making it, in the end, all part of that same ocean. From the highest perspective of the universe, you have chosen your family/lineage in order to experience, understand, expand, and, most importantly, heal the generational trauma by healing yourself. The timeline, parents, and culture were all pre-birth decisions and choices you made. This pre-birth decision binds your infinite soul with your physical body by your created soul contract. This contract includes all of what you pre intended to experience and try out on Earth. With, of course, the intention to forget all about the contract to make things even more exciting with a limited timeline (I.e., human life span) to experience and play. And as you may know now it's only on earth we have this construct with the dualities. Therefore, whatever you had put as "want to experience" inside your contract, you will first need to experience its other polarity, such as the negative, in order to recognize its positive. Just look at your life until now. The partner you chose, the life you chose, your family, your job, the culture, the traditions...and then compare ALL of that to what your heart, your intuition, is calling. Compare your experiences to your desires, wants, needs, and values. The rise of the highest self and the inner calling of what your heart is asking of you. That is all part of the choices and experiences you are having with this sacred temple of your human body and the life you are currently living on earth. Recognizing and connecting all the threads will make your life easier to understand. Your choices aligned with your heart will allow your entire life experience to be way more joyful, connected, and aligned with purpose. You will find more ease and meaning to your day to day, to your journey from then till now and what you still want to accomplish here on earth before your time runs out. This is where the rubber meets the road. Where one can be grateful for all the pain felt, for all the unwanted experiences. We can find meaning and understanding in everything that has been happening for us all along. Even if we could not understand other relationships around us, bonds being stronger or bonds being broken, it all had its specific reason and purpose to unfold the way it did. People coming into our lives, or people leaving...Outcomes unfolding and not that ultimately lead to even better-dreamed opportunities. This all points to a way larger picture of the cosmic web of the Universe and that there is a big thread and connection at the highest experience happening for everyone and everything involved from the start. These are your road maps to understand and go towards expansion. Ultimately, you came from one point of experience to see the inherent contrast between both states of both polarities. You are here on earth to play the games of the gods, and each experience is valuable information to bring back to you, back to the source. The laws of manifestations, magnetization, and attractions are just universal laws in order for you to exchange and see what you can attract in this lifetime. Just like in video games, there are "cheat codes" that one could use to upgrade their life for their benefit and the fun of the game. In the same way, you came here to live the most beautiful, magical, meaningful, and purposeful life one could ever experience. To use the gifts you came here with, your innate, chosen, learned, or acquired talents of writing, singing, painting, or anything that drives your heart...you name it. Take what you love doing most in life and simply go do that. Breaking the glass ceiling, stepping out of modern slavery, and becoming limitless, infinite, and creative and let that creativity inspire you and drive you...The cherry on top of this magical cake of yours: if your passion involves being of service to others, to the world, the side effect of that can only be returned back to you, to receive abundance of love, health, and wealth. So why live in fear or in possible regret? Look at the projections from other people made upon you since you were a child; that happened for you up to this very day. Any problems, insecurity, anger, shame, or abandonment. That was never yours to believe or carry. Forgive them for all of that, and forgive yourself. We are all co-creators. The separation between you and any other human can be seen as an illusion. Looking at another human is just a mirror, as if you were looking at yourself that has chosen to live a different life, a different path. There is such sacredness and beauty in the recognition of the synchronicities connecting us all together with Mother Earth. Still, if it seems difficult to grasp or understand, just take a look at your hand right now. Let's dive into a final little exercise and connect the micro to the macro. Modify your breathing into a total of seven deep, long breaths, way slower than your usual breathing. Make the exhale longer than the inhale. Take it really, very deep and very slow as you are just looking at your hand. You can come back to this exercise as you contemplate your hand with gratitude (I.e., related to this little meditation and contemplation practice to what I'm about to explain as you keep reading). As you are looking at your hand, make a tight fist for a few seconds and re-open it slowly as you keep observing. Watch its color turn from white to pink again; watch how the blood flow comes out and back in. During this entire time, continue to keep breathing very slowly and deeply. Your blood, your cells are right there in front of you. But is it separate from you? Is that hand a separate entity on its own connected to you that is watching it? Or is this you in some different form? Each cell in your body works separately, intelligently on its own. Fifty trillion cells. But are they you? An entire ecosystem within all parts of the whole body. With your mind and your thoughts, you observe it, separate it, analyze it, recognize, contemplating as if it is all separate parts of you, or if the All is you...your heart, your lungs, your liver, all organs and glands, fluids and cells are all part of you; or are you? Separating them internally with the mind, yet they are part of the whole making you, You. This is the micro to the macro. How do you view the earth and its entire ecosystem with all its humans, nature, animals, all of it...? Can you now, start to connect the dots? Seeing the beauty in everything, we come here as babies, innocent and pure, to see the world again as a child, with amazement while being an adult is relieving. It is regaining a long-lost freedom from illusionary constraints. We are walking back toward our hearts and the pureness of just being. To quote Ram Dass, "We are all just walking each other home." And I believe home is towards the heart, home to infinite pure Love. That being said, follow your heart and your dreams and strive to live that joyful life that is meaningful and purposeful, no matter how that may look to you. I hope this book is your remembrance to take each lesson and ritual to own your life and alchemize the gifts of pain and suffering into Love, into birthing the new "you". So that whenever fear, anger or sadness come at you like a big wave, you can use that opportunity to surf on it instead of being crushed by it. Because the rules of the games are yours, and as you remember, so as you play. You are God. And it is You. By you being God, Love, Source, Infinite Consciousness, you are an extension of it...

The Universe is just you-inverse.

#

References and Attributions

Chapter 2: The term and works of Deconstruction firstly coined by French philosopher Jacques Derrida in the 1960s.

Chapter 3: Dr Maxwell Maltz studies in the 1960s on 21 days repeated behavior.
By James Redfield studies from the 1990s, quote: where attention goes energy flows
1955-1601 Quote by William Shakespeare hamlet play: To be or not to be, that is the question.

Chapter 4: Scientific research from Heart/mind coherence studies from Heart Coherence institute Boulder Creek California. Work that also inspired by scientists Dr, Joe Dispenza and Gregg Braden.
Albert Einstein skepticism about quantum mechanics in a letter 1947 to Max Born
1911 Ernest Rutherford pioneer studies for radioactivity, coined the empty space in atoms.

Chapter 5: 470 BC quote by Hermes Trismegistus "as above so below, as within so without, as the Universe so the Soul..."
Studies on atoms binding by P.h.D. Bruce H. Lipton

Chapter 6: 1994 Studies on water influence by Dr Masaru Emoto

Chapter 7: 500Bc - 200Ad Patanjali a Hindu sage wrote the yoga sutras

Chapter 8: Scientific research 1880 - 1882 Pierre and Jacques Curie conducting electricity with crystals, named since then piezoelectricity and pyroelectricity.

Primary work in Fibonacci number described by Indian mathematician Pingala 200BC, work then introduced in1202 by Italian mathematician Leonardo of Pisa (known as Fibonacci) in western European mathematics.
Research in astrology: work published 1982 by astrologer Joanna Martine Woolfolk (1940-2013)

Chapter 9: John Archibald Wheeler, American theoretical physicist, coined the word black hole. Studies, in journals about experiments of matter and space time and observer effect.
Research on epigenetics 1940 by British biologist Hal Waddington and 70s Dr Bruce Lipton cell biologist.
2005 National science Foundation published study on thoughts, quantity, repetition and quality of thought.
Studies on placebo and nocebo and Electromagnetic field (I.e: EMF) published in Scientific Journal Nature. Asbstract/Intro & Matherials and Methods

Chapter 10: reminder of epigenetic in-utero by researchers in ref in point Chapter 9
Studies on brainwaves Hans Berger 1929 and 1899 Ernest Rutherford
EFT technique studies, published 2018 Healthcare international, scientific, peer-reviewed journal

Chapter 11: Scott Turow author & lawyer quote: Who are we but the stories we tell ourselves, about ourselves, and believe.

Research done by the department of Evolutionary Genetics, Max Planck Institute for Evolutionary Anthropology and various institutes published in 2015, by Kuhlwilm, M., Gronau, I., Hubisz, M.

Research chromosome N2, FOXP2 gene, Dr. Stephen C. Meyer & physicist Gregg Braden

Teachings Hermetics: 1st century AD Hermes Trismegistus and Kyballion published 1908 by William Walker Atkinson, 1862–1932

Chapter 12: word psychedelic actually derives from ancient Greek "psihi" (I.e. soul) and "dilosi" (I.e. manifest); which makes the word: soul-manifesting

God Molecule 5-MeO-DMT term coined by Dr. Gerardo Ruben Sandoval Dr. and co-author PhD Martin W. Ball.

1931 British chemist Richard Manske first to synthesized DMT. In the year 2016 scientists Szabo & Frecska published a research in the institute of clinical medicine, Oslo Norway; found that DMT produced in the human pineal gland had a protective compound related to treat neuron-inflammation and enhance neuron-protection, within dying cell tissues that were not enough oxygenated.

Stanislav Grov PHD, proposed that DMT is released in the pineal gland and could be activated by holotropic Breath-work

The psychoactive effects of LSD were first discovered in 1943 by Albert Hofmann at Sandoz Laboratories in the 1950s.

Researchers: James E., Robertshaw T.L., Hoskins M. and Sessa B. A study – trial experiment on psilocybin at Human Psychopharmacology Clinique

Buddhist Medical Practices in the Assimilation of the Opium Poppy in Chinese Medicine during the Song Dynasty (960–1279)

Song dynasty, Kaibao bencao; published in 974, stated, that it is prescribed for improving the circulation of qi (life force or in yogic traditions "Prana"

Chapter 13: term used Disneyland Park, ownded/founded by Walt Disney and Roy O. Disney

Nasseim Haramein studied physics and mathematics for more than 30 years, calculated that protons within atoms appear to have the same mass as the universe

1998 Blavatsky Helena one of the first to coin the term "highest self"

Ram Dass, quote "we are all just walking each other home"

www.ingramcontent.com/pod-product-compliance
Lightning Source LLC
Chambersburg PA
CBHW051508120626
46551CB00012B/819